Fresno

HEARTBEAT
OF THE VALLEY

Fresno

HEARTBEAT
OF THE VALLEY

INTRODUCTION BY
Cruz M. Bustamante

ART DIRECTION BY
Enrique Espinosa

SPONSORED BY
*The Fresno
Chamber of Commerce*

TOWERY PUBLISHING, INC.

**URBAN
TAPESTRY
SERIES**

TOWERY
PUBLISHING, INC.

Table of Contents

© JONATHAN POSTAL

© JONATHAN POSTAL

FRUITSTAND 200 FEET

IT IS AN HONOR TO WELCOME you as you take a glimpse at the heartbeat of California's Central Valley: Fresno.

By Cruz M. Bustamante

Although my duties as lieutenant governor usually keep me at the state capital, my heart is always in Fresno. My family and friends live in Fresno; it is my home. Before being elected to my post, I was an assemblyman for California's 31st State Assembly District, which includes Fresno.

© CAROL D. HUNT

Fresno is unique in that it has a metropolitan glare, while still maintaining a small-town familiarity. Time and again, I hear stories about people who grew up in Fresno, left to establish themselves professionally, and later returned to settle down. The same can be said in my case, although I have yet to settle down permanently. However, I return to Fresno when I get caught up in the political whirlwind and need a respite.

Fresno has many components that distinguish it from other cities.

One of the first things that you notice about Fresno is the abundant cultural diversity. More than 100 languages are spoken by ➥

© JONATHAN POSTAL

the students in the Fresno Unified School District. Fresno also hosts many sizable events and festivities throughout the year that celebrate our diversity. These events include the weeklong Hmong National New Year Celebration, the ¡Viva El Mariachi! Festival, and the blessing of the grapes at St. Paul Armenian Church.

Another distinction brought by way of diversity exists in Fresno's artistic community. Fresno is home to the African American Historical and Cultural Museum, as well as Arte Américas, demonstrating the community's support for efforts that bolster cultural awareness. Finally, like other metropolitan cities, Fresno has a

© TIM FLEMING

Chinatown. Near downtown, Chinatown hosts the annual E Street Fair and serves as the premier exhibit for traditional Chinese and Japanese architecture, including the Fresno Betsuin Buddhist Temple.

F resno also prides itself on its commitment to preserving and restoring the city's historical buildings, structures, and monuments. They serve as a testament to the importance of tradition in this town. Downtown Fresno, in particular, is one of the focal points of restoration and revitalization efforts. The Fresno Water Tower, built in 1894, is one of the first structures to benefit from such efforts. The facade has been completely restored to its original form, and the tower now serves as a museum. ➥

© JONATHAN POSTAL

SECURITY BANK

Welcome

Downtown
Fulton Mall

I, too, have many memories of a time when downtown Fresno was the place to be. I remember my family packing into our car and heading downtown to the Fulton Mall for an afternoon of food, folks, and fun. Back then, huge department stores like Gottschalks, Roos-Atkins, and JCPenney lined the outdoor mall. The emphasis was on something for the whole family. If it wasn't shopping, you could go catch a movie at the Crest Theater. And if that wasn't enough, there was also Woolworth's, the store that had everything—even a fountain shop! As time went on, businesses headed north, leaving behind desolate buildings with sporadic tenants. However, thanks to the commitment to restoration and revitalization, the area

◆ © RICHARD CUMMINS / PHOTOPHILE

is slowly turning over a new leaf—and the recent unveiling of a $35 million exhibit hall doesn't hinder those efforts, either!

◆ © RODNEY GAVROIAN

Unlike some other cities, Fresno's revitalization efforts have been quite successful. One success story is the Tower District. Anchored by the Tower Theater, this district clearly stands out despite its small size. The Tower District has a reputation for successfully bringing people together from all walks of life for a plethora of reasons, whether it be Mardi Gras, Farmers Market, or Halloween. As for the rest of the year, residents and visitors never encounter a shortage of things to do here. They can gather at any of the many coffee shops, dance at several nightclubs, or shop for anything from cigars ◆▸

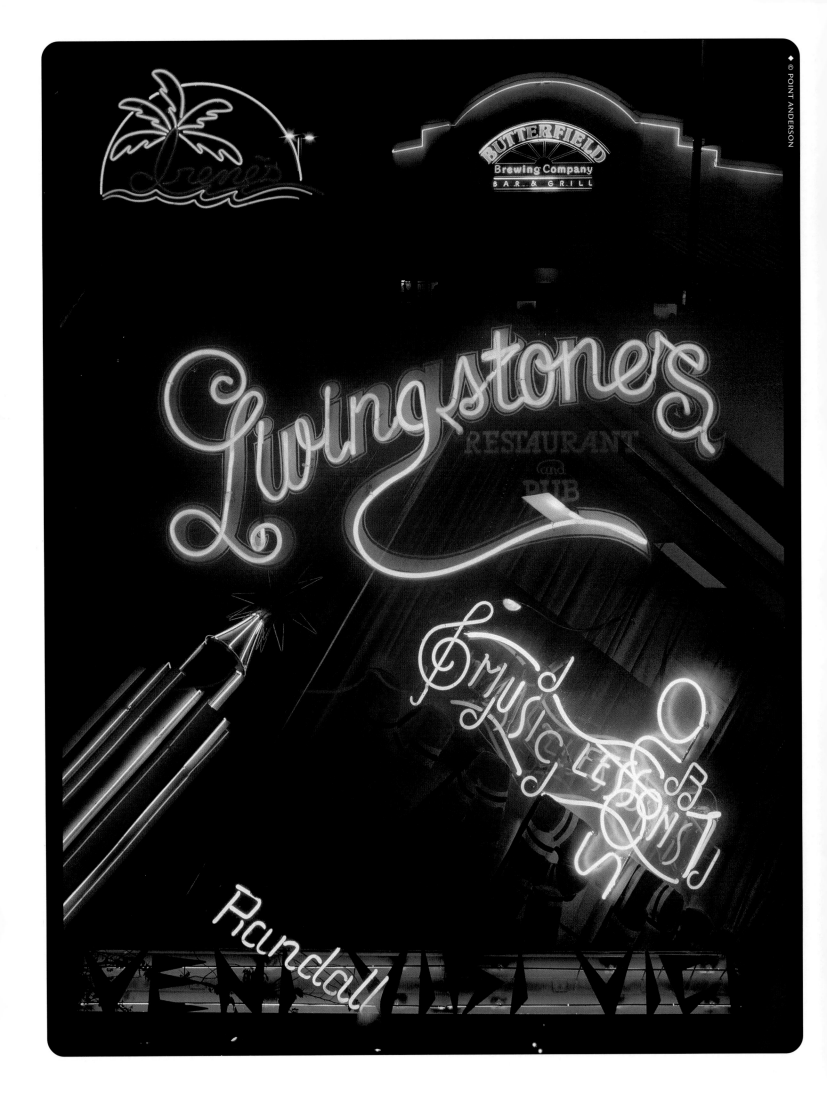

to retro clothing or vinyl records at the specialty shops along Olive Avenue. On any given day, you can see people rollerblading, young parents pushing strollers, and even men sporting Mohawks. On one occasion, I even saw a man walking his iguana on a leash! Regardless, the Tower District is a thriving mecca of individualism and independence, all made possible by determined residents who were not willing to stand by and witness the decaying buildings or the demise of the theater for which the district is named.

Now, just as the Fulton Mall and the Tower District represent a Fresno of yesterday, there is an abundance of places that represent

© TIM FLEMING

the Fresno of today. One of those places (and one of my particular favorites) is the River Park Shopping Center, on the north end of town. Like the Fulton Mall in its heyday, River Park offers a family atmosphere with something for everyone. There are plenty of big-box stores, many places for fine dining, and a huge, 21-theater cineplex. However, my favorite place at the outdoor center is also the one that gives Fresno another fine distinction: the IMAX theater. Fresno is one of only some 60 cities in the country with such a theater. I recently took my family to see a movie on the five-story-tall screen, and I can assure you that my six-year-old daughter, Marissa, perfectly summed up my opinion of the IMAX experience: "Very cool!" ➺

© JONATHAN POSTAL

Although technology has taken over most of the state of California, Fresno has remained true to its agricultural roots. Agriculture is one of the top sources of income in the area—from the field worker to the rancher. Fresno is the breadbasket of the world. A prime exporter in the raisin, grape, citrus, and cotton industries, Fresno also is a large supplier in the cattle and dairy industries. In addition, agriculture thrives on a different level at California State University, Fresno (Fresno State). There, agriculture is one of the more popular majors on campus, and students are coordinating with majors in other arenas, seeking to reinvent many means of farming.

Contrary to popular belief, Fresno has more to offer than just agriculture. It is home to a thriving arts scene. On any given day, the Fresno Metropolitan Museum offers exhibits on robotics, Christmas trees from around the world, and even world-famous Fabergé eggs. The same can be said for the Fresno Art Museum. If you prefer audio art to visual, Fresno also has a symphony orchestra— the Fresno Philharmonic—and a renewed interest in the opera.

The Saroyan Theatre is a common stop for professional traveling theater companies, although Fresno has three live theater companies of its own: Theatre 3 Repertory Company, Theatre J'Nerique, and the Good Company Players. Roger Rocka's Music Hall, located in ➥

the Tower District, is home to the Good Company Players and has served as the training ground for several Tony Award winners and nominees, like three-time Tony winner Audra McDonald.

Although Fresno has yet to receive the official nod, I consider it to be an All-America City. Fresno has an Air National Guard base and training grounds for the armed forces.

On a lighter note, Fresno also hosts several of the state's beauty and scholarship pageants, including Miss California, Miss California USA, and Miss Teen California USA.

© TODD WARSHAW / ALLSPORT USA

Fresno is also an All-America City when it comes to sports. The Fresno public embraces collegiate sports, whether it be Fresno State or Fresno City College. On autumn weekends, Fresno State fans, known as the Red Wave, converge upon Jim Sweeney Field at Bull-dog Stadium for football action. Fresno also has professional sports teams, including a Triple-A baseball team, the Fresno Grizzlies, and a hockey team, the Fresno Falcons.

© JONATHAN POSTAL

I hope that you have enjoyed my take on Fresno and all that the heartbeat of the Central Valley has to offer. It is my hope that my description of the city's essence has piqued your interest about the place I call home. ❧

While you glance through the following pages at pictures of Fresno, it should be interesting to note that in the coming years, Fresno will have more than half a million residents.

Nevertheless, I know that the city will maintain the small-town familiarity that another Fresno native, Pulitzer Prize-winning author William Saroyan, wrote about in the short story "Uncle Aslan":

"There were alien places in the earth, far from our valley, places we knew by name through print, Chicago, Philadelphia, New York, London, Paris, Berlin, Vienna, and there was also our small city

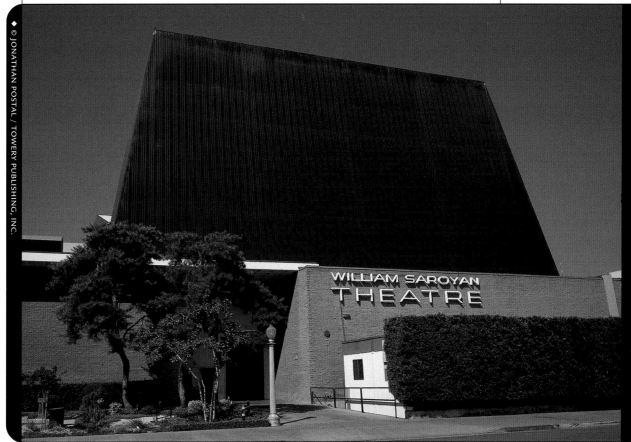

◆ © JONATHAN POSTAL / TOWERY PUBLISHING, INC.

with its familiar streets and structures, with its country roads and vineyards and trees and our sky and the faces of our people. It was good to be on the great earth and to have a specific place in which to be known and loved...." ❖

◆ © MICHAEL KARIBIAN

FOR THOSE IMMIGRANTS who have made their way to California in search of a better life, Fresno has the word "paradise" written all over it.

AS THE LEADING AGRI-
business area in the
nation, Fresno County
produces more than 250 different
crops—most of which can be
found on display at the popular
Clovis Farmers Market (OPPOSITE)
and the Fresno Farmers Market
(ABOVE).

ONCE DESERT, THE FRESNO countryside has been irrigated successfully over the past 50 years, resulting in some of the most fruitful land in the world. More than 7,500 farmers harvest their crops in the area, creating an annual gross revenue of $3.5 billion.

SERVING UP A HEALTHY slice of education, the Pizza Farm (ABOVE) has become a popular field trip for Fresno students. The circular farm's eight, wedge-shaped plots contain wheat, tomatoes, dairy cows, pigs, olives, peppers, herbs, and beef cows—all of the ingredients needed to make a pizza. Combine with a glass of wine from one of Fresno's vineyards (OPPOSITE) and you've got a great meal.

TO BEE OR NOT TO BEE: For Fresnans, this question has an easy answer. From beehives and bee costumes to bee buildings and bee planes—a replica of the famous 1930s-era Gee Bee racer—life in Fresno is definitely not for the birds.

WILDLIFE OF ALL KINDS have found loving homes in the Fresno area. Chaffee Zoological Gardens (BOTTOM AND OPPOSITE) is internationally recognized for breeding endangered animals, while the Sierra Endangered Cat Haven (TOP) is dedicated to the conservation of cats in their natural habitat.

THE SERENITY OF THE KOI pond at Fresno's Shinzen Japanese Garden (OPPOSITE AND ABOVE) attracts myriad visitors seeking a quiet atmosphere.

A fishy business of another sort, the landmark Central Fish Co. in Chinatown (PAGES 48 AND 49) provides locals with a variety of aquatic treats.

With an emphasis on local products and a seasonal menu, partners Adams Holland and Tim Woods (OPPOSITE, FROM LEFT) have garnered wide support for their restaurant Echo, located in Fresno's Tower District. Whether your taste buds crave the five-course meals served at the Santa Fe Basque Restaurant (TOP) or the juicy flavors of a good, old-fashioned backyard barbecue, the area offers a variety of culinary choices.

THERE'S MORE THAN ONE way to squeeze a grape: There's wine and then there's Grape Puffs, a new food product from Fresno-based Sierra Nut House and Fresno State. Carter Clary (LEFT), director of the Dried Foods Technology Laboratory at the university, joined forces with the local natural foods company in hopes of demonstrating the commercial value of the MIVAC—microwave/vacuum— a machine developed after a four-year research project, and funded in part by McDonnell Douglas. The MIVAC removes nearly all the water from a wide range of products, without damaging flavor or color.

I N FRESNO, A NIGHT OUT on the town can lead to plenty of smiles, plenty of fun, and sometimes a rousing song or two. From garden parties (PAGES 56 AND 57) to karaoke bars, the city's nightlife is alive and well.

THE FAMILIAR, DOWN-HOME atmosphere of local favorites Elaine's Cafe and Coney Island Restaurant draws a crowd of loyal diners.

NEVER TOO YOUNG OR too old to look suave and debonair, local residents head to the Clovis Barbershop for a bit of coiffing. Be prepared to wait in line, however: At the only barbershop in town without a telephone, there's no such thing as an appointment.

WITH A HEADS UP TO THE world of the *très chic*, Fresno's many beauty emporiums provide residents with an extensive selection of ways to fashion their curls or polish their nails. And in a local mall, two style setters demonstrate how to hold a model wedding (PAGES 64 AND 65).

S OME THINGS NEVER
change: There's still
nothing better than
going for a cruise in a custom
car with your sweetie (PAGES
66–69).

EVA AND HAROLD MATHEWS (TOP AND OPPOSITE TOP) put their hawg-wild tendencies to good use in 1952 and opened Mathews Harley-Davidson. Today, the store is known for its impressive collection of the historic bikes.

Botanica San Judas Tadeo
Productos Mexicanos de Botica

CR

Mexican Drugs Products.

Acapulco Jewelers

Acapulco Jewelers
Credito facil y
no se le cobra interes
Perforacion de oidos   3.95
denitas   3.00
apartado
le

BOTANICA
AN JUDAS
TADEO:
+VELADORAS
+INCIENSOS
+ACEITES
+HIERBAS
MEDICINALES

THE DIVERSITY OF NA-
tionalities found in Fresno
ensures an array of shops
and specialty stores catering to the
city's multiethnic residents.

SEVERAL AREA SCHOOL districts provide a Grade A education for students in the valley. The Fresno Unified School District, which is the state's fourth largest, includes some 90 schools and more than 78,000 pupils.

RESNO CITY COLLEGE was the first community college established in California. Today, with more than 18,000 students, the school offers courses in 100 different majors.

NOT ONES TO BE CHAINED down, Fresno teens head to the Tower District for a night of fun and frolic.

OSTS TO FILMS AND LIVE vaudeville in their heyday, the old movie houses of Fresno have not been abandoned or forgotten, but cherished for their beautiful architecture. The Crest and the Wilson theaters (TOP AND BOTTOM) have been converted to places of worship, while the Warnors Theatre (OPPOSITE BOTTOM) has taken to the stage, hosting many big-name and local musical acts. The Tower Theatre (OPPOSITE TOP)—the focal point of the lively Tower District—is one of the few that have remained true to their reel roots, offering children's classic movie matinees during the summer.

VISITORS TO TABLE MOUN-
tain Casino in nearby
Friant don their poker
faces for a night of high stakes—
and maybe a jackpot or two.

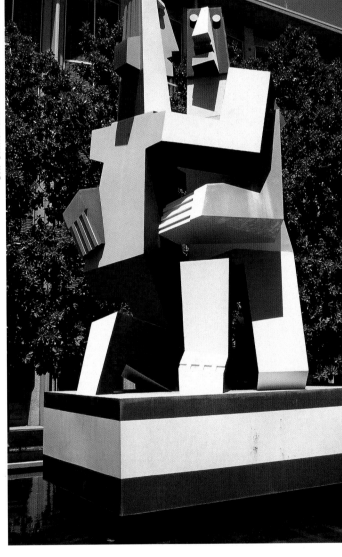

G REETING CITY RESIDENTS at every turn, outdoor statuary flourishes in Fresno. Works of renowned sculptors, such as the late Varaz Samuelian (OPPOSITE), cover the valley with their uniquely beautiful interpretations of life. Multimedia artists Robert Ogata (PAGE 86) and Margaret Hudson (PAGE 87) use their visions of Fresno's landscape and people to inspire their creations on the canvas and in clay.

FRESNO'S MUSIC SCENE plays on an international stage due to the contributions of legendary musicians such as Harmonica Slim (OPPOSITE) and others who infuse audiences with their soulful tunes.

BANDS FROM ALL OVER the world recognize Warnors Theatre as an excellent venue. Built in the early 1900s as a movie house, Warnors still reflects the gran- deur of the golden era of film, and today stages a range of performances by groups such as the Gipsy Kings (ABOVE), precursors to the Latin music explosion.

Bailemos, dansons, balliamo: Fresno's diverse cultures all recognize the universal language of dance.

Since the days of Roy Rogers and his trusty steed Trigger, the life of the cowboy has been romanticized in song. The popular Fresno trio Sons of the San Joaquin (OPPOSITE) is hitting the right chords in the cowboy music industry, crooning ballads of life on the range.

WHOA, PARDNER! One of a handful of rodeos shown on ESPN, the Clovis Rodeo features seven categories of competition, including bull riding, calf roping, and barrel racing.

WHETHER ON A JUNGLE gym or a gate at the ro– deo, sometimes you just gotta hang in there.

CALIFORNIA DREAMIN'
is becoming surreality:
Gray skies form a celes-
tial canvas for Fresno's industrial
landscape.

HE LINEAR SHADOWS OF Fresno's silos and wine distilleries lend a subtle beauty to otherwise desolate sights. There are days when that really matters.

WINDOWS TO THE PAST, Fresno's old buildings stand as reminders of the city's roots in High Renaissance and baroque architecture.

THE STAINLESS STEEL and glass sleekness of the Fig Garden Financial Center (OPPOSITE) and the Fresno City Hall (PAGES 107-109) are representative of the city's achievements in modern architecture. Now considered one of the most beautiful buildings in Fresno, the City Hall was initially met with controversy and some ill sentiment.

E VER MINDFUL OF FRESNO'S progress, an inner-city development committee— cochaired by Councilman Harry Perea (OPPOSITE, BOTTOM LEFT)— meets regularly to discuss improving housing in the city.

EPITOMIZING THE CLEAN lines of downtown, the $28.5 million Fresno Convention Center Exhibit Hall (ABOVE) represents the city's commitment to revitalization.

MANSIONS SUCH AS THE Meux Home (LEFT) AND the Kearney Mansion (OPPOSITE TOP) have been restored and converted to museums, giving visitors a glimpse into the private lives of some of the city's most prominent citizens. Other architecturally interesting properties are called home by many Fresnans.

IN 1906, BALDASARE Forestiere began digging a cellar for a cool place to rest and to store food. Not stopping at one room, he continued digging until his death in 1946, creating a labyrinth of underground niches, passageways, and courtyards that at one point covered 10 acres. Now listed on the National Register of Historic Places, Forestiere Underground Gardens continues to awe visitors with its painstaking construction. Grandnephew Andre Forestiere (OPPOSITE) joins family members in the quest to understand his famous uncle's motivation.

BATH

To a metal tank above ground, he attached a hose. He then filled the tank with water, which the sun would heat.

After bathing, he pulled the plug and the water would flow down and into a lower layer of sand. Thus there was no standing water.

BATH ALCOVE

RUB-A-DUB-DUB, TWO men and their tubs: It's only fitting that the bathroom in the Fresno home of raisin baron Martin Theodore Kearney (ABOVE) be preserved for posterity. After all, it was Kearney's belief that, if properly irrigated, the fertile San Joaquin Valley would prove ripe for agricultural endeavors. The rustic surrounds of Baldasare Forestiere's underground bath alcove (OPPOSITE) pale by comparison. But none of the more modern conveniences matches the thrill of a summer plunge in the Kings River (PAGES 120 AND 121).

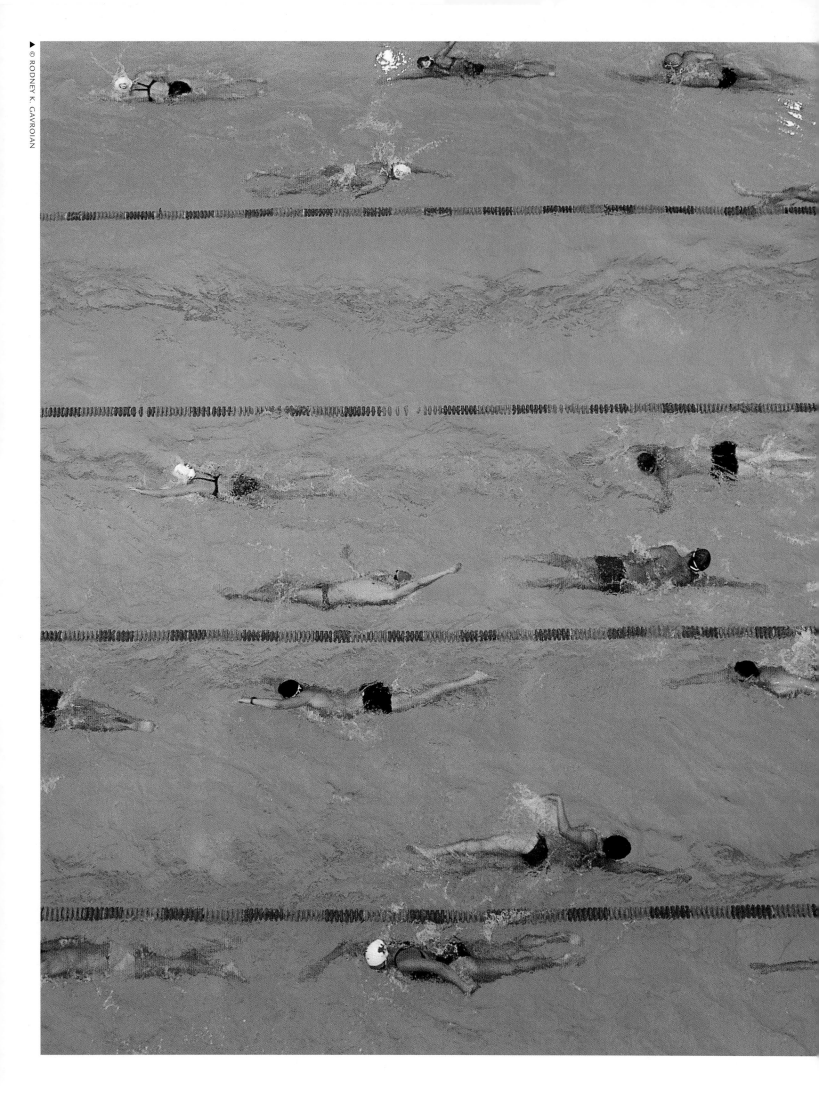

122

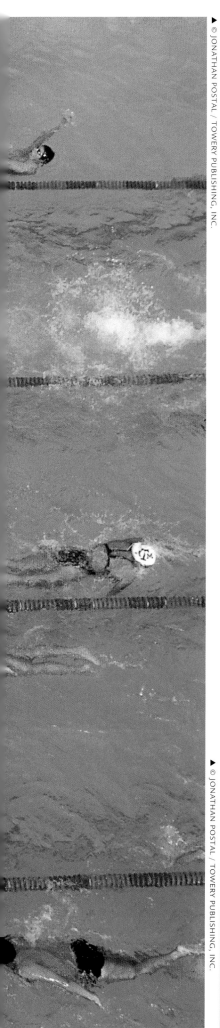

IN 1998, CLOVIS WEST High School hosted the U.S. National Swimming Championships (OPPOSITE). The competition attracted more than 1,000 of the nation's best swimmers, including Olympians and Olympic hopefuls. Fresnans not prepared for the rigors of competitive swimming head to Wild Water Adventures (LEFT) for a splashing good time.

HELD ANNUALLY AT Huntington Lake, the High Sierra Regatta attracts the nation's best racers.

The event's popularity stems from the lake's constant, strong wind, which will pack a powerful punch in your sails.

LOCATED JUST AN HOUR TO the northeast of Fresno, beautiful Yosemite National Park features 1,200 square miles of land set aside for preservation in 1890. Inside the park's boundaries, three groves of giant sequoias and some of the country's most dynamic waterfalls entice thousands of visitors annually.

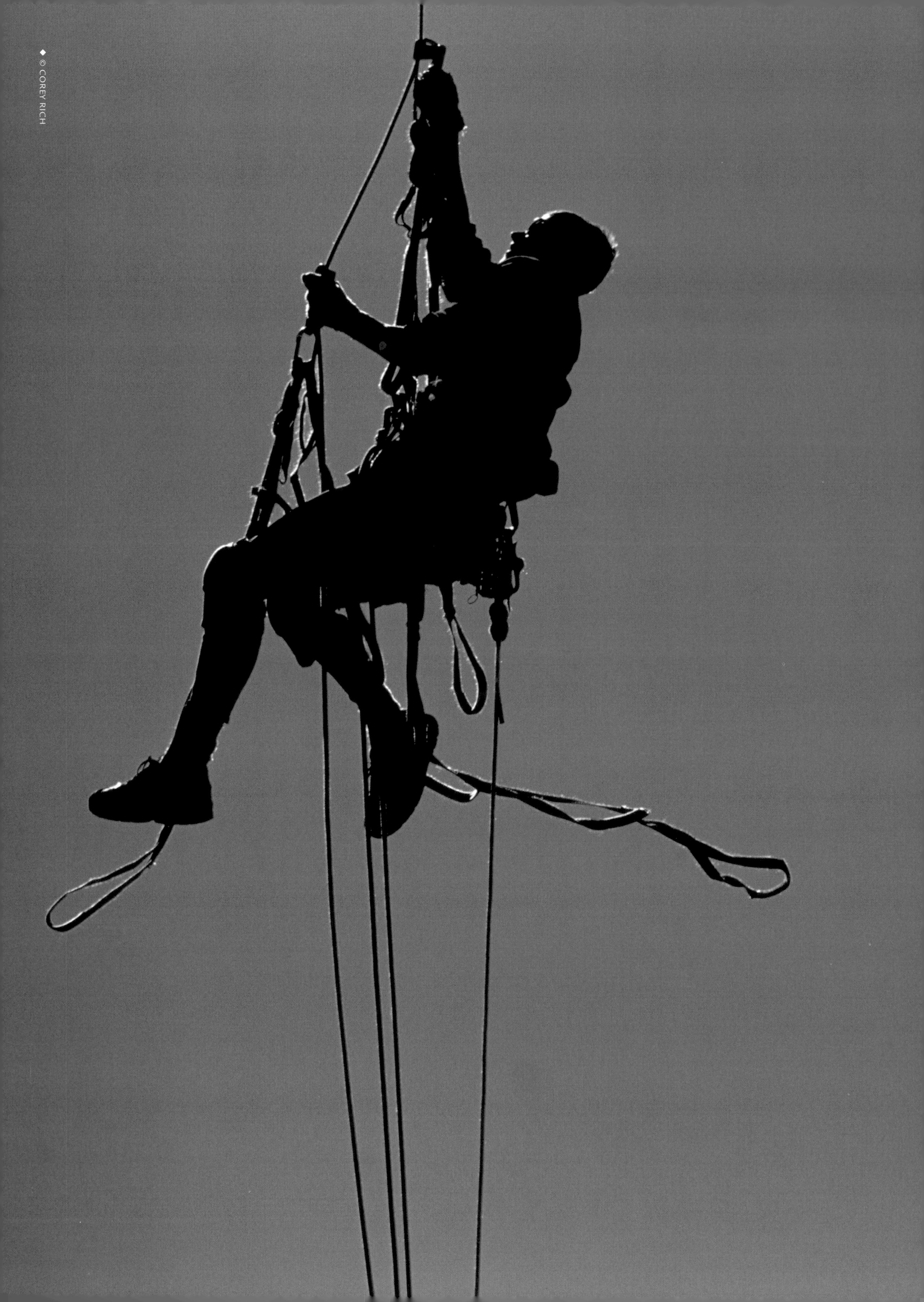

© COREY RICH

I N Fresno, scaling new heights comes naturally. Los Angeles school principal Bob Porter—a climber since his teens—and climbing partner Martin Avidan (PAGE 132) conquered Yosemite's El Capitan—a four-day, 2,500-foot ascent of the world's largest monolith—in an effort to raise funds for a new sports and recreation center on the campus of an L.A. school. But, whatever your motivation, jamming the crevices of central California's rock formations and mountains becomes a rush for any adrenaline junky (PAGE 133).

LIFE GOT YA' FEELING ALL gridlocked? Take a hint from members of the younger generation, who seem to be getting their spirits lifted at a local bounce house.

T HE RINGSIDE GYM IN Fresno, owned and operated for 15 years by Paul Carmello, offers a safe haven for teens seeking refuge from the street. In addition, the hangout serves as training grounds for local kickboxing champion Lisa Smith (LEFT), as well as former national amateur boxing champion Ray Lovato (RIGHT). The city's 11,300-seat Selland Arena (OPPOSITE) is also home to professional boxing and a variety of other sporting events.

BATTERS HAVE BEEN UP since 1998 for the Triple-A Fresno Grizzlies, led by president and CEO John Carbray (OPPOSITE). More than 350,000 fans flocked to Beiden Field to witness the team's opening season.

KNOWN AS THE RED Wave, fans of the Fresno State Bulldogs attend the university's football games en masse, cheering with a ferocity of dynamic proportions. Members of the Bullard Magic girls' soccer team, like their older counterparts, also tend to be goal oriented.

For Fresnans with an ax to grind, the Loggers Jamboree celebrates the fine art of logging. Lumberjacks competing in the annual event in North Fork test their skills in such activities as log burling, power sawing, and ax throwing.

NSIDE AND OUT, FRESNANS condition themselves with vigor, whether pumping iron—or the ubiquitous cell phone.

IT'S NO LAUGHING MATTER when one of Fresno's finest catches you speeding. But for native son Gary Scelzi (LEFT), fast driving has become a way of life. The former Top Fuel champion won the first two races he entered, making him the first driver in any of the National Hot Rod Association's professional categories to accomplish that feat.

CONSTRUCTION OF NEW housing—as well as of the shopping areas and businesses that come with growth— continues at a steady pace in the valley, where the Fresno-area population is expected to reach nearly 1 million by 2010.

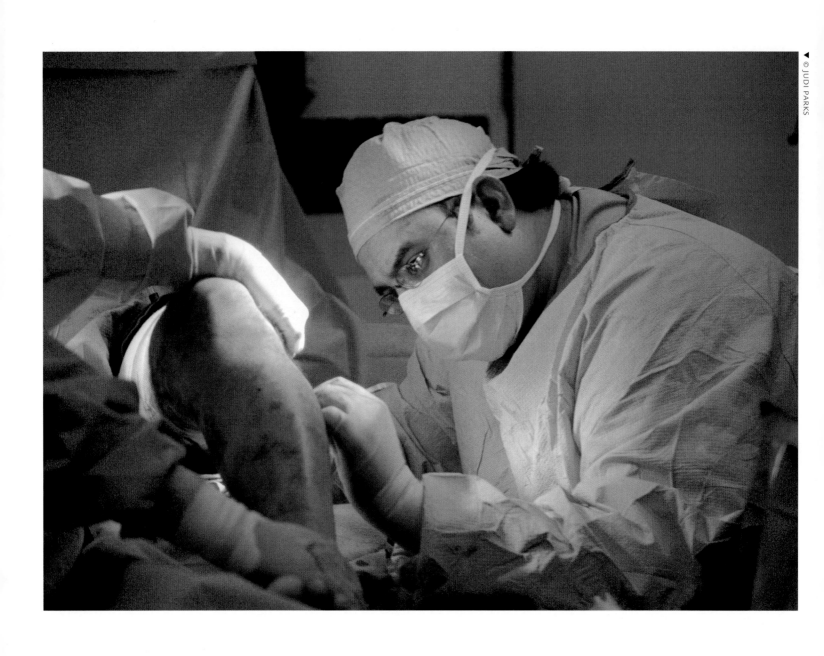

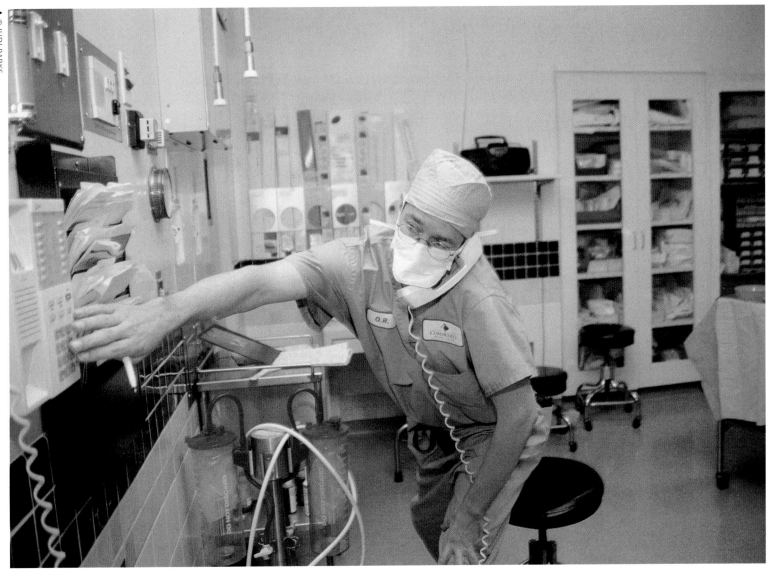

WITH NUMEROUS MEDICAL centers and hospitals, including the innovative Fresno Surgery Center (OPPOSITE), Fresnans can be assured of receiving the absolute latest in health care technology.

THE SKYWATCH OPERA-
tions unit of the Fresno
Police Department (LEFT
AND TOP) keeps Fresno safe and
sound by patrolling from a bird's-
eye view. Through rigorous
training, the Fresno Fire Department (BOTTOM) also does its duty
to protect citizens of the San
Joaquin Valley.

F OR AN UP CLOSE EX-
perience with unique
aircraft, Fresno residents
head toward local air shows,
which display such silver birds
as the British Spitfire, the stealth
fighter, and the F-16 named,
appropriately, *Spirit of Fresno*.

GRAVEYARD MARKERS honor Fresno's departed. The final resting place for area veterans, Liberty Cemetery (ABOVE) remembers those who faithfully served the nation, placing American flags at their burial sites each Memorial Day.

A LANDMARK IN DOWNTOWN Fresno, St. John's Cathedral has been undergoing major renovations for almost a decade, with restoration efforts funded by the city's vast Catholic population. Though much smaller in size, the Holy Trinity Armenian Apostolic Church—led by the Reverend Vahan Gosdanian (OPPOSITE)—caters to an equally devout and loyal congregation.

THE DIVERSITY OF FRESNO'S population is evident in the variety of religious groups that can be found in the region. The largest mosque in the San Joaquin Valley, Masjid Fresno is led by Iman and Shiekh Muhammad Sidahmad (ABOVE).

Fresno's Hmong community, one of the largest in the United States, celebrates a nine-day New Year's festival every year at the Fresno Fairground (LEFT). Under the watchful eye of spiritual leaders such as Reverend William Masuda (OPPOSITE) of the Fresno Betsuin Buddhist Temple, Fresno's Asian-Americans honor centuries of tradition.

The past, present, and future of Fresno is depicted on murals throughout the city, including the outer walls of the Hugh M. Burns State Building (PAGE 165).

CHICANO
YOUTH
CENTER
2 Miles

STATE OF CALIFORNIA

▲ © LUPE C. MORA

FAST APPROACHING A new era of growth and prosperity, the heart of the San Joaquin Valley sounds a steady and triumphant beat.

Profiles in Excellence

A look at the corporations, businesses, professional groups, and community service organizations that have made this book possible. Their stories—offering an informal chronicle of the local business community—are arranged according to the date they were established in Fresno.

ALLIANT UNIVERSITY ❖ AT&T ❖ BAKER, MANOCK & JENSEN, ATTORNEYS AT LAW ❖ THE BIG FRESNO FAIR ❖ BOYLE ENGINEERING CORPORATION ❖ CALIFORNIA STATE UNIVERSITY, FRESNO ❖ COMMUNITY MEDICAL CENTERS ❖ ECONOMIC DEVELOPMENT CORPORATION ❖ EDUCATIONAL EMPLOYEES CREDIT UNION ❖ FASHION FAIR MALL ❖ FLOWAY PUMPS ❖ THE FRESNO BEE ❖ FRESNO CHAMBER OF COMMERCE ❖ FRESNO CITY COLLEGE/REEDLEY COLLEGE/STATE CENTER COMMUNITY COLLEGE DISTRICT ❖ FRESNO PACIFIC UNIVERSITY ❖ FRESNO UNIFIED SCHOOL DISTRICT ❖ FRESNO YOSEMITE INTERNATIONAL AIRPORT ❖ GAP INC. ❖ GRUNDFOS PUMPS CORPORATION ❖ GUARDIAN INDUSTRIES CORPORATION ❖ GUNNER & ANDROS INVESTMENTS ❖ INTERNATIONAL ENGLISH INSTITUTE ❖ KAISER PERMANENTE ❖ KJEO CHANNEL 47 ❖ KJWL 99.3 ❖ KRAFT FOODS–CAPRI SUN ❖ LONGS DRUG STORES ❖ MANCO ABBOTT, INC. ❖ PACIFIC BELL ❖ PACIFIC GAS AND ELECTRIC COMPANY ❖ PAYROLL PEOPLE INC. ❖ PELCO ❖ PRODUCERS DAIRY FOODS, INC. ❖ THE RADISSON HOTEL & CONFERENCE CENTER ❖ SAINT AGNES MEDICAL CENTER ❖ THE SAN JOAQUIN SUITES HOTEL ❖ SAN MAR PROPERTIES INC. ❖ SIERRA TEL COMMUNICATIONS GROUP ❖ SUN-MAID GROWERS OF CALIFORNIA ❖ SUNRISE MEDICAL/QUICKIE DESIGNS ❖ TABLE MOUNTAIN RANCHERIA CASINO AND BINGO ❖ THOMCO INSURANCE ASSOCIATES, INC. ❖ UNITED ASSOCIATION OF PLUMBERS, PIPE AND REFRIGERATION FITTERS ❖ UPRIGHT, INC. ❖ VALCOM TECHNOLOGY CENTER ❖ VALLEY CHILDREN'S HOSPITAL ❖ VALLEY LAHVOSH BAKING COMPANY ❖ VALLEY SMALL BUSINESS DEVELOPMENT CORPORATION ❖ WILLEY TILE COMPANY ❖

SURROUNDED BY A TREE-FILLED CAMPUS, THOUSANDS OF ACRES of farmland, and a supportive and enthusiastic community, Reedley College offers a quality education to more and more students each year. Located at the foot of the Sierra Nevada, and just minutes south of downtown Fresno, the college has a unique blend of urban refinement and rural values.

Reedley College got its start in 1926 through an act of the board of trustees of the Reedley Joint Union High School District, establishing a junior college as part of the school district's program. In 1964, after an extensive study of the college district organization, aided by statutes mandating the inclusion of high schools in community college districts, the State Center Community College District (SCCCD) was established, joining Fresno City College with Reedley College. Today, Reedley College educates more than 4,500 students each year. The Reedley site is one of only 12 community colleges in California to provide on-campus housing.

EDUCATION THAT COUNTS

Students at Reedley College can earn a two-year associate degree, prepare for a transfer to a four-year university, or gain skills for immediate employment in many exciting and growing fields.

"We see mostly students from rural high schools and this college is a great place to make the transition to attend a university," says Thomas Crow, president of Reedley College. "We offer a comprehensive curriculum based on traditional subjects, as well as leading-edge technology."

Reedley College's offerings range from traditional classrooms and science laboratories to state-of-the-art occupational training facilities. Operating on an 18-week semester system during the spring and fall terms, the college has flexible class schedules designed to meet the needs of working adults. Courses are offered at the main campus in Reedley, and also cover the rural area, with seven community campus locations. Four-, six-, and eight-week summer sessions also make it easier to gain an education and the skills needed to be successful.

"Our popular programs get results because we have great instructors and the top-of-the-line equipment they need," says Crow, who speaks highly of the Aviation Maintenance Technology Program. The program is one of only 21 certified programs in California, and has its own 20,000-square-foot aviation hangar, which enables students to experience hands-on knowledge.

Other programs offering real-life experience include the Registered Dental Assistant Program and the Equipment Technician Program, which features a 2-to-1 lab-to-lecture ratio, as well as training in agriculture, construc-

tion, and material handling equipment and on-highway trucks.

The recently added—and highly acclaimed—Computer Graphics Program features a state-of-the-art computer lab, and will expand with growth and changes in the industry. Agribusiness, animal science, forestry, general agriculture, landscape horticulture, mechanized agriculture, natural resources, and plant science are some other popular offerings.

"People need to realize we offer a quality education in a beautiful and safe environment," says Crow. "Students aren't a number here. It is very personalized, and if someone needs help and is struggling, they see someone who knows their name and their situation."

For Reedley College, such effort has been the key to success.

REEDLEY COLLEGE IS LOCATED AT THE FOOT OF THE SIERRA NEVADA AND IS BORDERED BY THE BEAUTIFUL KINGS RIVER.

THE COLLEGE OFFERS INSTRUCTIONAL OPPORTUNITIES THAT RANGE FROM TRADITIONAL CLASSROOMS TO STATE-OF-THE-ART OCCUPATIONAL TRAINING FACILITIES (LEFT).

THE COLLEGE'S LOCATION PERMITS THE NATURAL SURROUNDINGS TO BECOME PART OF THE LEARNING ENVIRONMENT (RIGHT).

ROWING IN POPULARITY EACH YEAR, THE STATE CENTER COMMUnity College District (SCCCD) gives residents of the Central San Joaquin Valley an opportunity to receive an affordable, quality education. The SCCCD has its beginnings in a 1961 law creating junior college districts in California. Originally called the State Center Junior College District, the SCCCD encom-

passes 5,400 square miles of the San Joaquin Valley and was approved by Valley voters in 1963.

From the campuses of two primary colleges—Fresno City College and Reedley College—and three North Centers—Clovis, Madera, and Oakhurst—students of all ages can pursue a college education, make changes in their professional careers for more lucrative vocations, or prepare to advance to a state university or college upon receiving an associate of arts or associate of science degree.

"Community colleges, in general, should really serve the community's specific needs," says Interim Vice Chancellor Terry Kershaw. "That is the beauty of the SCCCD system. We have one of the best open-door policies in the world, and everyone is welcome to come and learn."

As a result, annual enrollment is increasing at the primary colleges and at the North Centers, which showed an overall enrollment increase of 25 percent for full-time equivalent students in the fall of 1999.

THE NORTH CENTER CAMPUSES

Current enrollment for the North Centers is more than 4,000 students. The centers employ 25 full-time faculty and more than

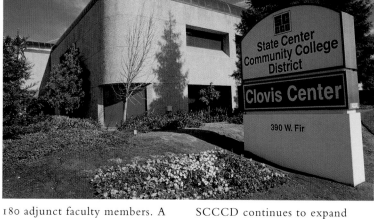

180 adjunct faculty members. A combined total of nearly 380 courses are taught, including short-term and weekend classes. Students can also take courses transmitted by computer from the other centers through SCCCD's Distance Learning Program.

Considered full-service campuses, the handicapped-accessible North Centers include a bookstore, library, cafeteria, and day care facility. Financial aid and counseling services are also available. In addition, the three centers provide five instructional computer labs housing 118 computers, with 30 additional computers in the libraries, giving the centers a 1-to-27 ratio of computers to students.

Because of its commitment to serve the students of the district,

SCCCD continues to expand services at the North Centers. Located on 114 acres on Avenue 12 at the edge of the city of Madera, the Madera Center includes a permanent Student Services building and portables. Construction of the first permanent academic and administration building will be completed by August 2000. At the Oakhurst Center, approximately 50 class sections each semester are available to students for general education and transfer programs. Currently located in the central business district of Oakhurst, the district is preparing plans to develop the 2.7 acres of property adjacent to the Oakhurst Center.

A PROMISING FUTURE

SCCCD's long-term goals for the North Centers are to eventually develop the sites into full-service community colleges. In the meantime, the campuses upgrade their facilities each year in different areas, working to meet the demands of the growing population and increasing enrollment.

"Our main goals remain the same," says Kershaw. "We will work to help transfer students move forward in their education and to help the students who seek a vocational career succeed. Mainly, SCCCD will continue to work for the communities."

THE RAPIDLY GROWING CLOVIS CENTER—PART OF STATE CENTER COMMUNITY COLLEGE DISTRICT— MAINTAINS A FRIENDLY, PERSONALIZED ATMOSPHERE.

MADERA CENTER STUDENTS ENJOY A BREAK BETWEEN CLASSES.

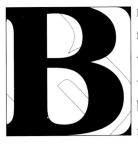

BENEATH THE HOT SUMMER SUN OF THE SAN JOAQUIN VALLEY, THE farmers of Sun-Maid Growers of California work to supply the world with a natural treat—sun-dried raisins—delivered in the widely recognized box with the smiling maiden and her red bonnet. Receiving and processing more than 100,000 tons of raisins annually, and reaching sales of more than $200 million each

year from its state-of-the-art facility in Kingsburg, California, Sun-Maid recently celebrated its 88th anniversary with continued growth and innovation.

Woven into the agricultural history of the San Joaquin Valley, Sun-Maid was established in 1912 by a group of raisin growers proposing what is still a successful grower-owned cooperative. "Being grower-owned is not only unique for such a large company, but it also shows we have dedicated farmers," says Sun-Maid Chairman Jon E. Marthedal. "Many farmers have been with the company for years, generations of families committed to producing the best-quality raisins and to advancing the industry as a whole."

RICH VALLEY HISTORY AND SOIL

A popular story of the industry's beginning tells of a heat wave that hit California in 1873, drying the grapes on the vine and threatening the farmers with potential economic disaster. Refusing defeat, resourceful growers took the sun-ripened grapes to San Francisco and sold them as Peruvian Delicacies. The debut of the raisin won the city over, and the growers returned with renewed prosperity and a unique industry.

By the early 1900s, a group of these visionary growers founded the grower-owned cooperative initially called the California Associated Raisin Company. Hoping to capture the magic and simplicity of their popular product and to create an exciting and memorable marketing image, the co-op took a new brand name in 1915—Sun-Maid. The company grew quickly, and opened a 187,000-square-foot processing plant in Fresno in 1918. It would be Sun-Maid's home for the next 46 years. As the 1960s approached, Sun-Maid began looking at upgrading its processing

plant, and decided to build a new plant between the cities of Selma and Kingsburg. The new facility quickly gained a reputation as the most modern raisin packing plant in the world.

MOVING FORWARD

Today, Sun-Maid distributes raisins in a wide variety of packages, from half-ounce, miniature boxes to 1,100-pound bins. The company's primary products are the Thompson Seedless natural sun-dried raisins and golden raisins, as well as Zante Currants, the dark, tiny raisins with a tart, tangy flavor.

Sun-Maid also markets a full line of dried fruit products ranging from apples and apricots to peaches and figs, as well as other dried fruit mixtures. Sun-Maid's brand licensing business segment continues to grow with a diverse product base of raisin bread, English muffins, chocolate-covered raisins, raisin oatmeal cookies, muffins, and fruitcake. Sun-Maid's original grower-member cooperative structure continues intact.

The company is still owned by its grower-members, which today number some 1,200 raisin farmers who produce one-third of the California raisin crop. Sun-Maid distributes its products throughout the United States, Europe, and the Pacific Rim, where the recognizable trademark of the maiden in the red bonnet assures quality in every package. "We are proud of being The World's Favorite Raisin," says President Barry F. Kriebel. "Sun-Maid has always been and will always be a significant part of the economic development of the Valley. It is a company that customers have trusted for more than 88 years, and we'll continue to earn that trust."

BESIDES PRODUCING THE WORLD'S FAVORITE RAISIN, SUN-MAID GROWERS OF CALIFORNIA LEADS THE INDUSTRY IN THE MARKETING OF ITS FULL LINE OF DRIED FRUIT AND BRAND-LICENSED PRODUCTS.

California State University, Fresno

CALIFORNIA STATE UNIVERSITY, FRESNO SERVES AS AN INTEGRAL part of the diverse tapestry that is Central San Joaquin Valley. Fresno State is about culture, history, tradition, community, and education. Respected as the preeminent regional university in Central California, it is highly esteemed for offering quality education, having a diverse student population, pro-

viding exceptional scholarship, and maintaining a leadership role in the cultural and academic motivation of students and the community.

With an enormous amount of activity in innovation, renovation, and state-of-the-art programs and equipment, as well as an overwhelming outpouring of spirit and contribution from the community, the university is moving ahead with a clear vision for the future. Fresno State has researched and developed its Vision for the 21st Century: A Plan for Excellence, a new strategy designed to continue the university's many successes. After looking at the needs of its students and community, Fresno State is ready to meet the many challenges of the 21st century. These challenges include cultural changes and population growth, increased demand for higher education, and the emergence of a global community.

"Our plan for the future reflects a deep commitment to strengthening our academic programs," says President John D. Welty. "It's imperative that we always address the new challenges of our students, faculty, and community, and that we also keep our focus. We're striving to grow even stronger through an emphasis on assessment and accountability, and through applied research that directly aids the communities of Central California."

Recognizing the important role a university plays in a specific region, Fresno State seeks to stay abreast of the growth and changes in the agricultural heartland, which is rapidly developing into a large and industrious metropolitan area. With the assistance of multiple task forces, the university has established a varied list of goals essential to meeting the challenges and opportunities lying ahead. It has already made many of these goals a reality, including the Smittcamp Family Honors College. With the construction of the Smittcamp Alumni House and Downing Planetarium, Fresno State has increased its ability to meet community needs. The continued and diligent work on numerous renovations to the infrastructure of the university adds to tradition and builds for the future. The

university is well on its way to accomplishing its ambitious goals.

A TRADITION OF BEAUTY AND EXCELLENCE

Established in 1911, Fresno State comprises 1,410 acres and is known as one of the oldest and most prestigious of the 23 campuses in the California State University (CSU) system. Today, the main Fresno State campus, formally dedicated as an arboretum, hosts more than 18,000 students annually in its 47 major buildings. Connected by tree-lined sidewalks, the 327-acre main campus greets students with glowing colors from the Chinese pistachio or exotic specimens of the bunya-bunya tree and features more than 4,000 trees of 85 different species. Working side by side with the community, the university's arboretum is home to Tree Fresno, a community organization dedicated to the planting of more trees, both on and off campus, and whose membership includes many alumni, students, and faculty members.

Once inside the classroom, students are guided by outstanding and motivated professors, approximately 85 percent of whom are tenured and hold doctoral degrees in their areas of study. The faculty includes many nationally and

internationally recognized researchers, artists, and educators who are experts in their fields.

Accredited by the California Board of Education and the Western Association of Schools and Colleges, Fresno State offers 56 bachelor's degrees and 40 master's degrees. It also has a doctoral program in educational leadership, offered jointly with the University of California. In addition, the university is privileged to offer students one of the primary training facilities for teachers in the state and the nation.

Fresno State has been honored with numerous awards and distinctions for various academic programs, including a fourth ranking for best

value among regional colleges and universities in the western United States by *U.S. News & World Report.*

DYNAMIC ACADEMICS AND GROWTH

During the last years of the 20th century, the faculty, deans, directors, and staff of Fresno State have focused on improving the quality of academics. Under the leadership of a dedicated faculty, the university ended 1999 with a list of remarkable accomplishments, including completion of the General Education (G.E.) review; creation of a four-year, integrated liberal studies multiple-subject credential program; and

implementation of a number of projects addressing the state's teacher shortage. It also has realized a record-setting year in grants, contracts, and support for research.

In 1999, the University Grants and Research Office reported more than 200 successful grant awards totaling in excess of $17 million. That figure represented an increase of more than 30 percent from the previous year. Major grants contributed markedly to Fresno State's academic environment and to outreach potential, including grants from the U.S. Department of Commerce, National Science Foundation, National Aeronautics and Space Administration, U.S. Department of Agriculture, National Endowment for the Humanities, U.S. Department of Education, National Institutes of Health, and numerous other federal and state agencies.

"Fresno State has seen an incredible amount of participation and devotion from the community," says Welty. "There has been a resurgence of pride in the community and the university. Our alumni and volunteers demonstrate it in their renewed enthusiasm and activity. It's also evident in the many extraordinary contributions that allow us to improve the campus and its programs on so many levels."

With the implementation of an improved G.E. program, the university is pleased to offer students a more comprehensive academic curricula. The coherence of the G.E. program aggressively assesses the needs of each school and college.

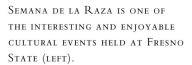

THE DOWNING PLANETARIUM FEATURES A COMPUTER-CONTROLLED SPITZ A3P STAR PROJECTOR.

SEMANA DE LA RAZA IS ONE OF THE INTERESTING AND ENJOYABLE CULTURAL EVENTS HELD AT FRESNO STATE (LEFT).

THE SID CRAIG SCHOOL OF BUSINESS IS RECOGNIZED AS HAVING ONE OF THE PREMIER BUSINESS PROGRAMS IN CALIFORNIA (RIGHT).

Beyond the important changes in the G.E. program, the university's eight schools and colleges have numerous accomplishments. Their achievements include new programs, funding, mergers, and accreditations, as well as increased enrollment and innumerable proactive changes in every department on different levels. "We have always believed in providing a hands-on experience for students," says Welty. "It's important for them to interact with their professors, stay involved in their education, and gain experience through internships, community service, applied research, and other forms of active learning. It gives them a competitive edge and the power to know they will succeed."

The College of Agricultural Sciences and Technology, for example, exceeded its targeted enrollment by 3.8 percent for a second year in a row. In addition, the National Association of State Universities and Land-Grant Colleges selected the school's Clinic Program to participate in a national exhibition. The school also is celebrating the establishment of the Department of Viticulture and Enology, which began in the fall of 2000. The university's own commercially licensed winery is the only one of its kind in the nation. It celebrates great success with statewide awards and is reaching out to the retail markets.

The College of Arts and Humanities faculty have published almost 30 books and nearly 90 articles. Together, the faculty and students have produced a wide variety of acclaimed presentations and creative performances. With support from every major art and performing arts organization in the community, the college hosts the CSU Summer Arts program, which is looking ahead to many successful years on the Fresno State campus.

The Sid Craig School of Business was acknowledged for its outstanding achievements, including accreditation on the first visit from the American Association of Collegiate Schools of Business, now known as the International Association for Management Education. The school's faculty accounted for 230 intellectual contributions, from professional presentations to journal articles and books. The Craig School has significantly increased its student internships and welcomed more than 70 firms to its second annual job fair.

The School of Education and Human Development exceeded its goal of meeting credentialed teacher quotas by increasing the number of full-time equivalent students. The school surmounted the challenge of creating a blended academic/professional preparation program in liberal studies. It also completed a smooth transition in administering the Joint Doctoral Program in Educational Leadership, previously administered by Graduate Studies.

The College of Engineering and Computer Science increased its enrollment and hosted a number of international visiting scholars, while the Computer Science Department developed an aggressive undergraduate outcome assessment plan.

The College of Health and Human Services worked on the implementation of its strategic plan and made great strides in using technology for instruction of 18 Internet courses.

The members of the College of Science and Mathematics have devoted many hours of production time to the state-of-the-art Central California Science Center (CCSC) and are planning for phase two of the project.

The College of Social Sciences made considerable progress developing a certificate program in American Humanics, which provides educational preparation for managing nonprofit organizations. The college also houses the Kenneth L. Maddy Institute for

Public Affairs, which provides a training institute for elected officials and internship opportunities for students.

SMITTCAMP FAMILY HONORS COLLEGE

A recent educational program at Fresno State is the Smittcamp Family Honors College. Attracting the finest students from across the state, the college offers a highly competitive and rigorous academic program to 50 high-achieving students each year. Funding was made possible by a generous donation from the Earl and Muriel Smittcamp family, owners and operators of the Wawona Orchards in Clovis, California. A businessman, farmer, and philanthropist, Earl Smittcamp has served on a number of school boards at the university, donating countless hours of time. The Smittcamps have four children, all graduates of Fresno State.

"This program is great for these students," says Dr. Stephen A. Rodemeyer, director of the Honors College. "It's challenging because it's designed to give them an opportunity to stretch themselves academically and individually among peers who are equally driven. The program focuses on the students' talent and success; they also enjoy general education and social affairs with the university population as a whole."

The main goal of the Smittcamp Family Honors College is to prepare graduates for leadership roles in the 21st century. Students attend two honors classes each semester during their freshman and sophomore years and sit in on weekly

PROFESSOR OF DESIGN MARY SCOTT SELECTS COLOR SWATCHES WITH A FRESNO STATE STUDENT.

colloquiums where they can share ideas and experiences. The students still attend regular courses with the general student population, including classes for their majors.

STRENGTH AND THE COMMUNITY

Recognizing the importance of a long-term relationship between the university and alumni, Fresno State has built the Smittcamp Alumni House, the largest such facility in the California State University system. A southern-style, 10,000-square-foot structure, the Smittcamp Alumni House features a warm, inviting atmosphere with garden vistas that create the perfect atmosphere to welcome alumni back to the university community. Included in the structure are offices, conference rooms, a kitchen, reception and social areas, and a library.

The Smittcamp Alumni House serves as the headquarters for the Fresno State Alumni Association, which was formed after the first graduation in 1912. Now with more than 100,000 graduates, the alumni association continues to promote the advancement of higher education at Fresno State and to enhance communication and fellowship among alumni and friends of the university.

Another addition to the campus is the state-of-the-art Downing Planetarium, the first building of the on-campus CCSC. Funded by a generous gift from retired Fresno physician Dr. Harold Downing and his family, the planetarium features a central theater that seats 74, a computer-controlled star projector, 29 slide projectors, a video projector, special theatrical lighting, and a surround-sound audio system.

THE SMITTCAMP ALUMNI HOUSE WELCOMES BULLDOG ALUMNI, CONFERENCE GOERS, DIGNITARIES, AND OTHER VISITORS TO THE FRESNO STATE CAMPUS (LEFT).

"It is a wonderful facility," says Dr. Steven J. White, planetarium director. "Fresno has waited a long time for a planetarium, so this is a great opportunity for the entire community. The Downing Planetarium is a versatile theater and provides teachers with a variety of programs for their students. We are open to schools and civic and religious organizations for field trips. We also provide special shows for the public."

The planetarium is a 4,000-square-foot building that houses the theater, a teacher training area, a work space for planetarium production, and eight computer workstations with network access. The staff at the planetarium produces modern planetarium programming for visitors, of whom 80 to 90 percent are expected to be school-age children.

Going beyond the stars, the planetarium also features shows on mythology and dinosaurs, as well as a number of other programs and permanent exhibits. A modern observatory equipped with a 16-inch, computer-controlled telescope is planned for construction behind the planetarium.

GO BULLDOGS GO

Fresno State's acclaimed athletics program provides opportunities for both men and women athletes to compete on a national level in more than a dozen sports. Men's sports include baseball, basketball, cross-country, football, golf, soccer, tennis, track and field, and wrestling. Women's sports include basketball, cross-country, equestrian, soccer, softball, swimming and diving, tennis, track and field, and volleyball.

The Bulldogs have a healthy athletics program that shows the school's competitive spirit. Athletics instill a sense of pride and confidence in the student body. They also present gifted individuals with an opportunity to earn a well-rounded education and provide a high level of community interaction. For the athletes, academic endeavors come first. One-fifth of Fresno State players make the Dean's List (which requires a 3.5 or higher grade point average) and a third of those on the Dean's List earn a 4.0.

A number of the university's programs have risen to national prominence, with the Bulldog women's softball team winning the national championship in 1998. A high point of the football program came in 1992, when Bulldog football players beat the heavily favored University of Southern California Trojans in the Freedom Bowl. Trent Dilfer—now a National Football League (NFL) quarterback—was at the helm; eight other players from his team went on to the NFL.

In addition, the men's basketball team boasts a National Invitational Tournament (NIT) championship, the women's volleyball team has made five postseason appearances in the last eight years, and other programs distinguish themselves locally, regionally, and nationally each year.

The success of the Bulldog athletic program and the intense community involvement are due in part to the Bulldog Foundation, which has led the nation in volunteer fund-raising every year since 1986. Since 1971, nearly $100 million

THE UPCOMING SAVE MART CENTER WILL SERVE AS HOME TO BULLDOG BASKETBALL, WHERE OUTSTANDING ATHLETES LIKE ALL-AMERICAN COURTNEY ALEXANDER WILL COMPETE. ALEXANDER EARNED RECOGNITION FROM *Bluechip* AND *Parade* MAGAZINES AND IS A NAISMITH AWARD CANDIDATE (LEFT).

THE CAMPUS MASCOT, TIMEOUT, SHARES A HUG WITH TWO BULLDOG FANS (RIGHT).

has been raised to benefit scholarships, recruiting needs, and facility improvements.

"The caliber of our players, their professors, and the athletic trainers is phenomenal," says Dr. Al Bohl, director of athletics. "Our community supporters—the Red Wave—and the Bulldog Foundation have all shown an outstanding amount of support for Fresno State. They know it's their college and their kids. It's easy to see how much everyone cares for these athletes."

The upcoming Save Mart Center offers one of the finest venues for sports, culture, and entertainment in Central California. Seating 16,000, the center will have the capacity to attract nationally prominent artists, sporting events, touring companies, and other attractions. It also will serve as home to Bulldog basketball and volleyball. "The Save Mart Center is designed to be a premier showcase facility for the entire Central California region," says Welty.

A BRIGHT FUTURE AHEAD

Fresno State hosts more than 200 student organizations, honor societies, fraternities, sororities, social groups, and cultural clubs, as well as numerous professional, vocational, and recreational organizations. Its calendar year is full of art exhibits, drama productions, concerts, recitals, movies, sporting events, and lectures. The University Lecture Series, for example, features internationally recognized political leaders, activists, artists, authors, and academics. The university also sponsors a variety of multicultural events that reflects the diverse student population, including African Peoples History Month, Amerasia Week, Heritage Week, Semana de la Raza, International Week, Women's Herstory Month, and the annual spring festival Vintage Days.

Whether students are attending classes on campus, looking for assistance, or seeking reentry information, the university provides numerous essential support services. Assistance programs begin during students' high school years and continue throughout their academic careers. Taking pride in the high level of interaction between stu-

dents, faculty, and staff, the university offers numerous programs aimed at enhancing the quality of education. Programs include career development and employment services, learning resource center access, an advising office, a summer bridge program, an educational opportunity program, university migrant services, a college assistance migrant program, Southeast Asian student services, a reentry program, a women's resource center, and services to students with disabilities.

Balancing exceptional educational opportunities with a caring campus environment, Fresno State

features state-of-the-art facilities, dynamic programs, and a reputation for providing one of the best educations available. Ranked in the top 10 percent by *Opportunity* magazine and rated number one among 16 of the CSU campuses for best graduation rate, Fresno State moves into the new century with a bright and strong future.

"This is an exciting time for the university," says Welty. "Fresno State hasn't seen this much activity since its relocation in the 1950s. We have a thriving campus that is growing even stronger. And everyone intends to keep it that way."

THE RED WAVE CONTINUED TO RIDE HIGH AFTER FRESNO STATE SOFTBALL'S NUMBER ONE RANKING AND NCAA CHAMPIONSHIP IN 1998.

FRESNO NORMAL SCHOOL HAD AN ENROLLMENT OF 150 STUDENTS WHEN IT BEGAN IN 1911. NOW, MORE THAN 18,000 STUDENTS ARE REGISTERED AT FRESNO STATE.

Table Mountain Rancheria Casino and Bingo

FOR THOUSANDS OF YEARS, NATIVE AMERICAN PEOPLE HAVE LIVED and traded in the Sierra Nevada foothills and mountains. In modern times, these native people have experienced a strong rebirth of their communities. Table Mountain Rancheria Casino and Bingo is a direct result of tribal self-determination, providing a degree of success unheard of in the Native American society in California.

Table Mountain Rancheria was founded in 1916, established by the U.S. government on 160 acres at an ancient village site in the Winchell Creek area near Friant. The people of Table Mountain Rancheria, along with many other smaller tribes in California, lost their federal recognition as Native Americans in 1959. After 20 years of struggle, that status was restored in 1983, and Table Mountain Rancheria Bingo began operation four years later.

FUN-FILLED GAMING OPTIONS

Today, Table Mountain features video gaming, card games, bingo, special events, and a full-service restaurant. Table Mountain welcomes more than 5,000 guests on average every day, and visitor satisfaction is the primary consideration of the staff. As the leading Indian gaming center in Central California, Table Mountain believes that guest relations are crucial to the success of the institution.

Visitors can choose from hundreds of video gaming machines or play card games such as Jackpot 21, pai gow poker, push nine, and Texas hold 'em poker. Bingo, the original attraction at Table Mountain, is as exciting as ever. Guests play bingo every Wednesday through Sunday night for big cash prizes and monthly giveaways. As an additional incentive to visitors of the facility, Table Mountain has a car-a-week giveaway and an annual house giveaway.

In addition to its many gaming options, Table Mountain Casino and Bingo features live music every night of the week, and the Eagles Landing Restaurant serves breakfast, lunch, and dinner to hungry patrons at any hour. The International Buffet—featured on Mondays and Tuesdays—features different foods from around the world. The Casino Trading Post stocks a large selection of Native American collectible artwork and handmade crafts to commemorate patrons' visits.

Table Mountain Rancheria plans to expand its guest facilities to accommodate new visitors, including adding new games, entertainment, and services. A museum showcasing native and settler history is also being built on tribal grounds. This project includes a reconstruction of Fort Miller, including the original blockhouse and various support structures, such as the officers' quarters and other buildings that were removed from the original site, now under Millerton Lake, and stored in a barn on Auberry Road for the last 50 years. All buildings will be constructed from as much of the original material as possible. The museum will have an extensive collection of archival photographs and artifacts, and will teach its visitors about the history of eastern Fresno County starting in the 1850s.

CONTRIBUTIONS TO THE COMMUNITY

With all of its success, Table Mountain Rancheria has not forgotten the community that supports it. "We place a high priority on community responsibility and awareness," says Robert Pennel, tribal anthropologist. The tribe's success is shared with employees, customers, and the public.

Table Mountain Rancheria's philosophy of reinvestment in the community provides enormous support to the area. Nonprofit organizations receiving contributions include the American Heart Association, the American Cancer Society, the American Diabetes Association, Central California Blood Center, Fresno Area Crime Stoppers, Valley Children's Hospital, and Central Valley Indian Health, to mention just a few.

Table Mountain Rancheria is also involved in many civic-minded pursuits, including the Fresno Zoological Society, the Kearney Palms Shopping Center, the Fresno City and County Historical Society's Greater Central Valley History Museum, the 1998 Civil War

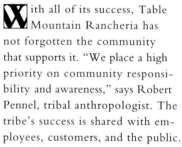

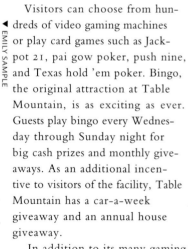

NATIVE AMERICANS ONCE PICKED CLOVER, A TRADITIONAL FOOD, WHERE THE TABLE MOUNTAIN RANCHERIA CASINO AND BINGO NOW STANDS.

EMILY SAMPLE

reenactment at Kearney Park, the Eastern Fresno County Historical Society, and the Sierra Mono Museum. Table Mountain Rancheria also provides an improved economic climate for eastern Fresno County, providing numerous jobs and business opportunities.

BENEFITS TO THE TRIBE

Since its beginning, the success of the casino has greatly improved the lives of the members of Table Mountain Rancheria.

Revenue from the casino has provided funds for a new medical center, where tribal members and employees receive medical, dental, and vision care. A new Tribal Learning Center sports after-school activities for tribal families. Tutoring services are also available. The Tribal Learning Center includes a fully staffed, state-of-the-art library.

Through all the improvements, the members of Table Mountain Rancheria hold fast to their culture. Privately, traditional ceremonies and gatherings take place today as they always have.

Table Mountain Rancheria embraces its rich heritage, and looks forward to building a bright future for the tribe, its employees, its visitors, and the communities of Central California. Growing from a spirit of self-determination, Table Mountain Casino and Bingo embodies a positive, all-encompassing cooperation in the true spirit of the Native American people.

VISITORS TO TABLE MOUNTAIN CAN CHOOSE FROM HUNDREDS OF VIDEO GAMING MACHINES AND A VARIETY OF CARD GAMES.

THROUGH ALL THE IMPROVEMENTS, THE MEMBERS OF TABLE MOUNTAIN RANCHERIA HOLD FAST TO THEIR CULTURE. PRIVATELY, TRADITIONAL CEREMONIES AND GATHERINGS TAKE PLACE TODAY AS THEY ALWAYS HAVE.

Valley Lahvosh Baking Company

IN THE EARLY 1900S, GAZAIR SAGHATELIAN SET OUT FROM HIS troubled homeland on a journey of freedom. He and his family immigrated to the United States desiring to bake in peace his wonderful Armenian breads. Gazair set up shop next door to his new home on M Street and Santa Clara in the heart of downtown Fresno, and in 1922, California Baking Company was born.

Today, the company is known as Valley Lahvosh Baking Company and is no longer just a corner bakery; it occupies the entire block. Valley Lahvosh has grown to offer a complete line of fine crackerbread, including its delicious trademark Valley Lahvosh crackerbread. Valley Lahvosh also produces Valley Peda, Gazair Saghatelian's signature hearth bread. Gazair created this delicate, old-world hearth bread, known for its light, airy texture and delicious taste, to commemorate his family's arrival in America. Valley Peda can only be purchased at the original bakery in downtown Fresno, and is made from a closely guarded family recipe, a true Saghatelian original.

"My grandfather was a strong, dynamic man who loved baking and his culture. He created Valley Peda to celebrate his new business, his family, and its new beginning," says Vice President Agnes Saghatelian. "He lived next door to the bakery and he baked with his brothers. Later, my uncle, Samuel Saghatelian, joined him in the business, followed

by my mother, Janet Saghatelian. Janet started helping when she was around 10. After Sam passed away in 1982, my mother became president of the company. She is a wise businesswoman who pursues her ideas and doesn't give up when she knows she is on the

GAZAIR SAGHATELIAN (TOP) FOUNDED THE CALIFORNIA BAKING COMPANY IN THE HEART OF DOWNTOWN FRESNO IN 1922 (BOTTOM). TODAY KNOWN AS VALLEY LAHVOSH BAKING COMPANY, IT IS STILL HEADQUARTERED IN THE SAME LOCATION.

right track. She always follows her heart."

Today, Janet Saghatelian oversees the management of the bakery. Her daughter, Agnes Saghatelian, a graduate of the Sid Craig School of Business at CSU, Fresno, runs the day-to-day operations, including the implementation of an aggressive marketing plan that reaches out to regional, national, and international customers.

THE HEART OF THE VALLEY

In 1983, Janet Saghatelian came up with the idea of a heart-shaped Valley Lahvosh crackerbread. A healthy bread, (low in fat and sodium and with no cholesterol), it seemed the perfect product for the health-conscious 1980s. Today, the popular kosher bread is the company's number one seller worldwide, and is considered its flagship product.

"To my mother, the heart represents not only health, but also family, love for the business, food, and people," says Agnes Saghatelian. "Many people told her it would be too difficult to make the crackerbread in a heart shape, but she was determined.

Nothing would stop my mother. Just like my grandfather, she has always worked very hard for the business, the family, and the community."

AWARD-WINNING VALLEY LAHVOSH

Having won many awards over the years for its quality products, Valley Lahvosh ended the 20th century with the honor of receiving the American Tasting Institute's (ATI) Best of Show award for its entire product line. The company received two of ATI's highest honors, having both its Valley Lahvosh crackerbread and Valley Wrap flatbread declared the finest made in America.

While the company's crackerbread is the heart of the business, Valley Lahvosh is also well known for another innovative product. During the early 1980s, Valley Lahvosh pioneered and ushered in the wrap sandwich trend with the invention of the Valley Wraps soft flatbread. Today, Valley Wraps is acknowledged as the finest flatbread for wraps, utilized by upscale restaurants, hotels, country clubs, and caterers alike.

Valley Lahvosh originally served primarily the Armenian community

in Fresno. But, as news spread of the delicious, healthy, and versatile Valley Lahvosh breads, people throughout the country took notice. Today, Valley Lahvosh products are found throughout the United States, Canada, Israel, and Japan. The company is proud to be still baking its products at its original location, with four distribution centers nationwide.

Even with all the success the bakery has achieved, it is still dedicated to its roots. "My family has always loved seeing the generations of customers come in over the years. In fact, the children and grandchildren of our original customers are now patrons of our bakery," says Agnes Saghatelian. "Our plans are to continue to bake the best breads possible, using only the purest ingredients. Valley Lahvosh will continue to grow until we are the number one supplier of specialty crackerbread and flatbread. I know my grandfather would be so proud to see what we have done to perpetuate and grow his bakery and his breads."

VALLEY LAHVOSH IS CURRENTLY OWNED BY GAZAIR'S YOUNGEST DAUGHTER, JANET (TOP), AND HER DAUGHTER AGNES (BOTTOM). JANET OVERSEES THE MANAGEMENT OF THE BAKERY; AGNES RUNS THE DAY-TO-DAY OPERATIONS.

The Fresno Bee

WHETHER READERS ENJOY IT IN THE MORNING WITH A HOT CUP of coffee or on the back porch after a hard day's work, *The Fresno Bee* has served the central California region with responsible, timely, and award-winning news reporting for more than 75 years. *The Bee* continues its rich heritage as a vital resource to generations of Fresnans, informing, empowering, and entertaining them as it grows.

"You'll see that *The Bee*, much like the fertile agricultural region in which it publishes, has evolved, grown, and replanted itself to remain current," says Publisher J. Keith Moyer. "And rest assured that such refinement of *The Bee* will continue as we enter our second 75 years of publication."

Now in its 78th year, *The Bee* has a daily circulation of more than 150,000 and on Sundays, more than 190,000. The numbers continue to increase over the years, as they have since the first publication.

In April 1922, The James McClatchy Co., publisher of *The Sacramento Bee,* and its editor, C.K. McClatchy, announced plans to publish a new newspaper and to build the headquarters at the southwest corner of Van Ness Avenue and Calaveras Street in Fresno. On October 17, 1922, the first edition of *The Fresno Bee* rolled off the press in its new home, starting a new tradition for 16,000 eager readers and many generations to come. Under the watchful eye of editor Carlos McClatchy, C.K. McClatchy's son, *The Bee* purchased *The Fresno Herald* in 1924 and *The Fresno Republican* in 1932, to become the city's only daily newspaper.

ON THE MOVE

Nearly five decades after printing its first paper, with a circulation of 120,000, *The Bee* was ready for a move. In 1970, *The Bee* published its first press run at the new building on E Street in downtown Fresno. The paper had been paralleling the growth of the city, and the new, 19-acre site allowed the addition of state-of-the-art equipment. Throughout the years, the newspaper had enlarged its type size, moved from an eight-column to a six-column layout, and progressed from a lead hot-type to a photo-based cold-type production. In the new facility, *The Bee* installed flexographic printing presses and new printing equipment. The operation began using water-based ink rather than oil-based ink, moving the newspaper into the future with an environmentally cleaner process.

The Fresno Bee is one of 20 newspapers owned and operated by The McClatchy Company. *The Bee*'s circulation encompasses six counties—Fresno, Kings, Tulare, Madera, Merced, and Mariposa—making it a preferred advertising tool. As it welcomes the hundreds of individuals who read it daily, the newspaper and its staff embrace the community. With countless hours, coverage, and donations provided to service clubs, nonprofit organizations, and community causes, the newspaper contributes much more than vital information.

As part of its extensive coverage and reach into Valley counties, *The Bee* is also affiliated with the community publications *Neighbors, Sierra Gateway Neighbors, The Clovis Independent*, and *Vida en el Valle*. For its Visalia-area readers, *The Bee* publishes *The South Valley Bee* every Friday.

"To see where the Valley might be headed tomorrow, it is necessary to see where we have been, to reflect on the hard work and dreams of those who came before us," says Moyer. *The Bee* exemplifies this philosophy and reflects on the past, while keeping an eye on the present and moving into the 21st century.

The Bee's Web site, fresnobee. com, is an important information tool for the newspaper and its readers as both enter the new millennium. The state-of-the-art site offers immediate access to local, national, and international stories, weather, sports, and features.

"Our enhanced Web site will, at the same time, be a bigger and better complement to the daily printed *Bee*, and a highly useful information source in its own right," says Moyer.

IN 1999, *The Fresno Bee* STARTED THE RENOVATION OF ITS NEWSROOM, COMPLETING THE PROJECT IN EARLY 2000. THE PROJECT, WHICH COST APPROXIMATELY $5 MILLION, INCREASED THE USABLE SQUARE FOOTAGE FROM 13,000 TO 23,000. PART OF THE RENOVATION TO THE NEW, STATE-OF-THE-ART NEWSROOM INCLUDED THE INSTALLATION OF THE UNISYS PAGINATION SYSTEM, WHICH ALLOWS PAGES TO BE SENT DIRECTLY FROM A TERMINAL TO A NEGATIVE FILM.

1929 — SAINT AGNES MEDICAL CENTER

1932 — PRODUCERS DAIRY FOODS, INC.

1934 — EDUCATIONAL EMPLOYEES CREDIT UNION

1934 — FLOWAY PUMPS

1942 — LONGS DRUG STORES

1944 — FRESNO PACIFIC UNIVERSITY

1946 — FRESNO YOSEMITE INTERNATIONAL AIRPORT

1952 — VALLEY CHILDREN'S HOSPITAL

1953 — KJEO CHANNEL 47

1966 — THOMCO INSURANCE ASSOCIATES, INC.

1969 — GUNNER & ANDROS INVESTMENTS

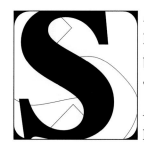

AINT AGNES MEDICAL CENTER'S COMMITMENT TO MEETING THE health care needs of central California is rooted in its humble beginnings as a 75-bed hospital at Fruit and Floradora avenues. This dedication was demonstrated back in 1929, when Saint Agnes opened its doors one day ahead of schedule, to save the life of a boy who needed surgery. Today, more than 70 years

later, Saint Agnes maintains its reputation for compassionate care and is highly respected by the community for its clinical and service excellence.

"We strive to be true to our mission of providing high-quality, compassionate care," says Sister Ruth Marie Nickerson, C.S.C., president and CEO of Saint Agnes Medical Center. "We have earned a strong reputation for service and we value our position within the community."

CLOCKWISE FROM TOP: "WE STRIVE TO BE TRUE TO OUR MISSION OF PROVIDING HIGH-QUALITY, COMPASSIONATE CARE," SAYS SISTER RUTH MARIE NICKERSON, C.S.C., PRESIDENT AND CEO OF SAINT AGNES MEDICAL CENTER.

IN 1999, SAINT AGNES WAS THE ONLY CENTRAL CALIFORNIA HOSPITAL HONORED AMONG THE TOP 100 HOSPITALS FOR CARDIAC BYPASS SURGERY IN AMERICA.

THE OUTPATIENT CENTER, ADDED IN 1993, HOUSES SURGERY SUITES, MAGNETIC RESONANCE IMAGING, OUTPATIENT LABORATORY SERVICES, RADIOLOGY, AND CRITICAL CARE.

RESPONDING TO NEED

Saint Agnes Medical Center's rich history traces back to the founding of the Sisters of the Holy Cross in Le Mans in 1841. Two years later, the Sisters made their way to South Bend. During the Civil War, they boarded the hospital ship *Red Rover* to care for wounded soldiers, making them the country's first navy nurses. Then, in 1894, a group of Sisters was called to Fresno to open a boarding and day school, Saint Augustine's Academy. Efforts to build another academy were redirected by Bishop John B. McGinley, who asked the Sisters to sponsor the first Catholic hospital instead—and Saint Agnes opened in 1929.

Since then, Saint Agnes has remained steadfast to its mission: "to be faithful to the spirit of the Sisters of the Holy Cross, to strive to witness God's love through excellence in the delivery of health services, and to be motivated by compassion and respect for the people of central California in responding to their health needs."

BUILDING A LEGACY

Once Saint Agnes Hospital opened, it quickly joined the ranks of nationally recognized facilities, accredited in its first three years by the American College of Surgeons.

In 1947, ground was broken for a three-story maternity wing, increasing the hospital's capacity to 150 beds. Within a few years, other additions were made, including a convalescent wing, new kitchen, chapel, and physical therapy department.

By the 1970s, new facilities were needed to meet increased patient demand, as was modern medical equipment. Responding again to the valley's health care needs, Saint Agnes purchased a 32-acre site in north Fresno for its new medical center. This move not only set the stage for state-of-the-art medical care in the valley, it also set the course for the city's expansion to the north. In 1976, the current Herndon Avenue facility opened and the name was changed to Saint Agnes Medical

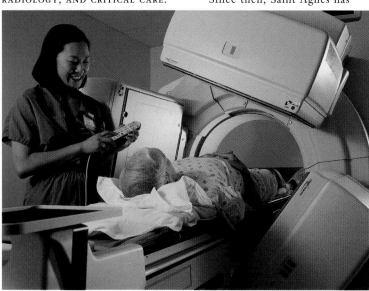

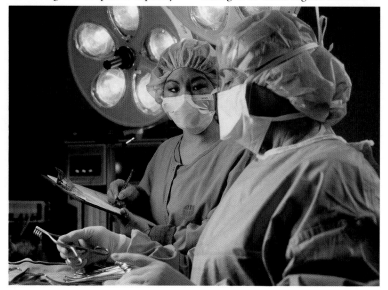

Center to better reflect the scope of services it would provide.

Saint Agnes celebrated another milestone in the early 1980s by opening a three-story wing that houses an additional 100 beds and specialized departments, including business office, data processing, volunteer office, discharge planning, social services, home care, education center, and hospice.

The Outpatient Center, added to the east side of the main building in 1993, houses surgery suites, magnetic resonance imaging, outpatient laboratory services, radiology, and critical care. The Medical Center's expansion across Herndon Avenue included the Cancer Center in 1993. This facility specializes in the compassionate care of cancer patients and their families, while combining the expertise of the area's outstanding physicians and the latest medical technology and treatment protocols.

FUTURE PLANS

Today, Saint Agnes Medical Center has 326 beds, a medical staff of 720, and 2,500 employees. Saint Agnes will welcome the new century by embarking on the most exciting expansion in its history. Plans include the addition of patient care beds and a cardiac wing to house cardiac catheterization labs and surgery suites, as well as an expanded emergency room with a chest pain observation unit. Long-range plans will encompass expansion and building renovation for other major services, such as general surgery, orthopedics, and neurology.

As Fresno's premier surgery facility, Saint Agnes is respected for its experience in a broad range of surgical specialties, including orthopedics, open-heart surgery, and neurology. In 1999, Saint Agnes was honored among the Top 100 Hospitals for Cardiac Bypass Surgery in America, making it the only central California hospital chosen as part of HCIA's Top 100 Cardiovascular Hospitals study, which identifies the best hospitals for open-heart surgery.

"This award clearly illustrates the caliber of heart care provided by our outstanding physicians, and our surgical and postoperative teams," says Nickerson. "It's a prestigious distinction, and one that we are very proud to share with the community."

In 1999, Saint Agnes was also named among 126 hospitals in 101 markets across the country as a 1999 Consumer Choice Award winner by National Research Corporation. This honor, granted by the nation's leading health care performance measurement firm, is based on consumer preference for the best hospital in their local area for quality and image. For the fourth consecutive year, the consensus among central California consumers was Saint Agnes Medical Center.

FULFILLING THE MISSION

Saint Agnes Medical Center's healing mission extends beyond its hospital walls to benefit the people of central California. Committed to building a healthier community, Saint Agnes invests in numerous causes and programs. Its investments are in the forms of time and money, and in the energy of its employees, physicians, and volunteers. Saint Agnes' commitment to the community is demonstrated by programs such as the Holy Cross Center for Women and the Holy Cross Clinic at Poverello House.

Holy Cross Center for Women provides a safe, clean haven for women and children in need. The center offers clothing, laundry facilities, educational skills classes, job and housing assistance, and referrals to alcohol/drug rehabilitation when necessary. Holy Cross Clinic at Poverello House is operated by Saint Agnes staff and volunteers who provide homeless or uninsured visitors medical and dental screenings, diagnoses, and treatments, as well as bilingual health education materials.

In addition to its outreach efforts to the underserved, Saint Agnes actively focuses on meeting the community's health needs. These include promoting breast cancer awareness and early detection, preventing domestic violence, increasing childhood immunization rates, and reducing the dropout rate among pregnant teens.

Saint Agnes Medical Center's vision of quality continues to define its growth. The organization will continue to meet its mission of compassionate care for years to come by combining state-of-the-art equipment and technology, the expertise of top-ranked physicians, surgical and cardiac facilities, and community outreach programs.

SAINT AGNES MEDICAL CENTER HAS REMAINED STEADFAST TO ITS MISSION, INCLUDING BEING "MOTIVATED BY COMPASSION AND RESPECT FOR THE PEOPLE OF CENTRAL CALIFORNIA IN RESPONDING TO THEIR HEALTH NEEDS" (LEFT).

HOLY CROSS CENTER FOR WOMEN PROVIDES A SAFE, CLEAN HAVEN FOR WOMEN AND CHILDREN IN NEED (RIGHT).

Producers Dairy Foods, Inc.

PRODUCERS DAIRY FOODS, INC. HAS BEEN DELIVERING THE FRESHEST dairy products to families throughout California for nearly seven decades. Moving into the 21st century with more than 300 employees, the company now serves more than 25 metropolitan areas, and is admired as one of the largest dairies in the western United States. ■ Headquartered in Fresno, Producers Dairy Foods has seven branch offices in San Luis Obispo, the Monterey Peninsula, the San Francisco Bay Area, Anderson, Sacramento, Ceres/Modesto, and Tulare.

A FAMILY BUSINESS

Established in Fresno in 1932, Producers Dairy Foods was incorporated by a group of ambitious men with a vision of packaging quality milk products for their community. Family-owned and -operated since 1949, Producers Dairy Foods began its expansion when Larry Shehadey purchased a major interest in the company. In 1951, he became general manager and began fulfilling his vision for the company. Providing the highest-quality product is Shehadey's priority, and he has steered the company toward many creative innovations used daily in the dairy industry.

"If you don't have quality, the customer won't want to buy or try your product," says Director of Sales and Marketing Dave Teeple. "In the dairy industry, you need to be able to provide your customer with constant quality, and at Producers Dairy the freshest product is the best product. We always work to produce the best."

EXPANSION AND INNOVATION

With Shehadey's firm commitment to quality, service, and freshness, Producers Dairy Foods decided to buy its own herds and its own dairy farms, from which the majority of its milk is processed. With Shehadey now serving as CEO for the company, and his son Richard serving as president and general manager, the company has maintained its focus on quality, while continuing to work on new innovations and waste reduction methods.

Beyond installing the latest in processing and sanitizing equipment, as well as a water purifying system, Producers Dairy Foods was the first company to employ a 100 percent refrigerated dairy fleet, and the first to use half-gallon and quart-size single-service packaging in the San Joaquin Valley. The company has also installed plastic bottle blow mold machines, which manufacture the Space Saver bottle, and has introduced a plastic pint-size milk bottle, the first of its kind in California.

"We really wanted to work on waste management and reduction for our community and the state," says Teeple. "We're now working on a mini-size, half-pint pouch that helps reduce waste by 70 percent and weight by 80 percent. You can fit 25 empty pouches in the old half-pint containers."

Giving back to the communities it serves has helped Producers Dairy Foods remain one of the few locally owned and independently operated dairies in California. The company has grown considerably since the early days of milk bottles and milkmen, and embraced its success by moving into an expansive new office in 1998, while remaining in its original location in the heart of downtown Fresno.

Now offering a complete line of dairy products, including ice cream, ice-cream novelties, butter, cheese, eggs, fruit juices, and drinking and spring waters, Producers Dairy Foods remains devoted to ensuring its customers' satisfaction. Looking toward the future, the company aims to stay true to its mission: "to produce the highest quality product at the lowest cost per unit while meeting customer expectations every time."

UNDER THE DIRECTION OF LARRY SHEHADEY (TOP, LEFT) AND RICHARD SHEHADEY (TOP, RIGHT), PRODUCERS DAIRY FOODS, INC. IS COMMITTED TO QUALITY, SERVICE, AND FRESHNESS. TO ACCOMPLISH THIS, THE COMPANY MAINTAINS ITS OWN HERDS AND WAS THE FIRST DAIRY COMPANY TO EMPLOY A 100 PERCENT REFRIGERATED FLEET (BOTTOM).

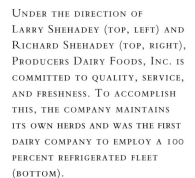

Educational Employees Credit Union

CELEBRATING MORE THAN 66 YEARS OF SERVICE, EDUCAtional Employees Credit Union (EECU) marked the end of the 20th century as the 78th-largest credit union in the United States, with assets of $613 million and a membership nearing 100,000. It also holds the distinct honor of being the largest financial institution based in the Central San Joaquin Valley and the 18th out of 700 credit unions in the state. Offering a full line of financial services to its members, EECU upholds a strong history of stability and continues to work toward a bright future in the new century.

Established in 1934 as the Fresno Teachers Credit Union with an initial investment of $200, EECU's success is due in part to its dedication to its primary mission: "to recognize and fulfill the financial needs of its members, school employees and their family members." In 1981, the organization's name was changed to Educational Employees Credit Union to better portray its relationship to its members and to the growing region it represents.

The credit union's membership now includes school employees in Fresno, Inyo, Kings, Madera, Mariposa, Merced, Monterey, San Benito, San Luis Obispo, and Tulare counties. EECU offers the latest in competitively priced financial services, lower loan rates, higher saving rates, and lower fees for financial services.

"Understanding and meeting the financial needs of our members is always our main goal," says Bruce Barnett, president and CEO. "We have an obligation to provide quality financial products and services, including expanding branches and automated services with the latest technology that is available."

Currently, EECU has 230 full-time employees and has recently expanded into a new, 42,000-square-foot operations center in north Fresno.

PARTNERSHIPS IN THE COMMUNITY

Over the years, EECU has enthusiastically supported educational programs and efforts of school systems, districts, and educational employees. In a partnership with the Fresno County Office of Education (FCOE), EECU has helped to create numerous programs that support and validate excellence in education.

Representing 34 districts and serving nearly 180,000 students, FCOE provides vital resources to districts, educators, and students in an effort to ensure that every one of its students achieves his or her academic potential. This county office is led by Dr. Peter G. Mehas, first elected superintendent of schools in 1990 and re-elected in 1994 and 1998. Mehas brings 38 years of experience to the position as a former teacher, principal, advisor to Governor Deukmejian, member of the State Board of Education, and member of the California Community College Board of Governors. Mehas says, "We support dynamic change, a multitude of partnerships, a vision for community involvement, and most importantly, student achievement. Our mission is to serve as a catalyst for students' success through our commitment to partnerships with school districts, parents, and public and private enterprise providing leadership for quality instruction and support programs into the new century and beyond."

BRUCE BARNETT, EDUCATIONAL EMPLOYEES CREDIT UNION (EECU) PRESIDENT AND CEO, AND DR. PETER G. MEHAS, FRESNO COUNTY SUPERINTENDENT OF SCHOOLS, ARE PICTURED HERE WITH THE CLEMENT RENZI SCULPTURE *Three Rs*, WHICH WAS COMMISSIONED FOR THE FRESNO COUNTY OFFICE OF EDUCATION TEACHER, ADMINISTRATOR, AND EMPLOYEE OF THE YEAR AWARDS.

THE FRESNO COUNTY ACADEMIC DECATHLON EXEMPLIFIES THE PARTNERSHIP BETWEEN EECU AND THE FRESNO COUNTY OFFICE OF EDUCATION (FCOE). MEHAS POSES WITH STUDENT DECATHLETES.

The County Office of Education acts as the intermediate level of the public education system in California and provides the necessary infrastructure for local schools and districts, offering a full range of programs and support services. These include professional training and staff development, curriculum, business and financial support, and health and pupil personnel services, as well as legislative and public policy leadership and advocacy.

ONE COMMUNITY WORKING TOGETHER

Just as it takes a village to educate a child, it takes a community working with its schools for a quality education. Partnerships are the glue that cement the children to real-life experiences and the schools to the community.

Together with the support of FCOE, EECU sponsors the Fresno County Teacher, Administrator, and Employee of the Year awards program. With participation and momentum for the awards growing each year, the program was established by Mehas and Barnett, who wanted to honor the county's top educators. Each year, superintendents submit nominees and a community-wide committee makes the final selection; all nominees, finalists, and winners are then honored at a Fall Awards Gala.

EECU is also a major sponsor of the Fresno County Academic Decathlon, hailed as the nation's most rigorous academic competition for high school students. FCOE also coordinates a number of other student competitions, including the Central California Regional Science, Mathematics, and Engineering Fair; College Night; Language Arts Festival; History Day; Young Author's Faire; Library Summit; Mock Trial; Mid-Year Youth Conference; Science Olympiad; Career Skills Olympics; Spell-Off; and Physical Fitness Pentathlon.

Educational Employees Credit Union acknowledges school administrators and their continued quest for quality education by supporting the Association of California School Administrators (ACSA), a professional association offering seminars and support to administrators throughout Fresno County.

Through numerous programs, partnerships, events, and sponsorships, EECU shares a vision with the community, along with a history of stability, strength, and integrity. Says Barnett, "This is the members' credit union and we will always work to be responsive to their needs and continue to grow and remain strong."

AS THE FRESNO COUNTY SUPERINTENDENT OF SCHOOLS, MEHAS VISITS CLASSROOMS REGULARLY, INTERACTING WITH BOTH STAFF AND STUDENTS.

THIS EDUCATIONAL EMPLOYEES CREDIT UNION BRANCH IS LOCATED AT SHAW AND VALENTINE AVENUES IN FRESNO.

Floway Pumps

ESTABLISHED IN 1934, FLOWAY PUMPS HAS BECOME AN international leader in the manufacture of vertical turbine pumps for industrial, municipal, commercial, and agricultural purposes. Blending theory and practice, the firm produces top-quality engineered products for a growing number of satisfied clients. ■ The company is known as an innovative competitor in design, installation, and service areas. Floway vertical turbine pumps are used for moving water, jet fuel, petroleum, and nuclear waste.

A PROUD PAST

Floway began as Fiese & Firstenberger Manufacturing, Inc. in 1934, and soon received recognition as a reliable manufacturer, delivering quality products and services. In the decade following World War II, the company concentrated on development and production, and created the Floway trademark in 1957. From this concerted effort came a highly

versatile vertical turbine pump used in a number of applications. To highlight this success, the corporation was renamed Floway Pumps, Inc. in 1967.

In 1975, a merger with Peabody International strengthened both companies. Through Floway's concern about the environment, pollution, and safety matters, the company received worldwide recognition as a quality manufacturer, and in 1992, was purchased by the Weir Group PLC of Glasgow. The Weir Group supports the innovative design teams and staff at Floway Pumps, and is pleased with the company's operations and high standards.

MANUFACTURING AND TESTING FACILITY

At Floway's main manufacturing facility in Fresno, the engineering teams work in a state-of-the-art, 200,000-square-foot production area, manufacturing and testing pumps. The company's open-door policy allows colleagues to utilize their talents to the fullest extent. Engineers work with the latest in materials—including nickel aluminum bronze—and with the specialized computer technology of solid modeling. The computer system allows Floway engineers to create three-dimensional models, and to rotate the projects in real time, making structural cuts and adding or subtracting materials.

Floway products can be found in a myriad of uses and places. From controlling the tumbling waters at Disneyland to manufacturing snow in Squaw Valley for great skiing to providing fire protection for the rapid transit system in Bangkok, Floway is known for quality-assured, safe, and durable products.

Throughout the state of California, the company's vertical turbine pumps are widely used in the agricultural and petroleum industries, as well as in providing municipal waters. Typical municipal applications include water supply from lakes, rivers, and wells; treated water filtration and effluent disposal; wastewater treatment and disposal; factory process and treatment; and numerous others. Floway's engineers can design and produce a pump to meet virtually any fluid moving requirement.

Known for its leadership in the industry, Floway was recently awarded a $2.9 million contract from the State of California's Department of Water Resources as part of the State Water Project. The project order includes eight pumping units ranging from 150 horsepower to 2,000 horsepower. The pumps, working together, will have the capacity to move more than 63 million gallons of water daily.

Proud of its success, Floway will continue striving to develop high-efficiency pumps for clients worldwide. Whether it is helping to keep the waters clean or moving fluid to create power, the company looks toward a bright future of providing top-quality pumping products and service.

FLOWAY PUMPS PRODUCED SIX 2,500 HORSEPOWER, 14,000 GALLON-PER-MINUTE PUMPS FOR THE JOHNSON COUNTY WATER DISTRICT IN KANSAS CITY, KANSAS (TOP).

FLOWAY PUMPS' MAIN FACILITY IS LOCATED IN FRESNO (BOTTOM).

LONGS DRUG STORES HAS SPENT MORE THAN 60 YEARS AT THE top of the nation's drugstore chain industry, and is moving strongly into the 21st century with a rich history built on traditional values. "We like to take things on a day-to-day basis, but we realize we have to work toward a bigger picture," says the company's vice president and Central District manager

Sal Petrucelli. "Everyday, we strive to treat our customers, employees, vendors, and community in general with the utmost respect and dignity."

With this vision and commitment serving as the cornerstone of the company's growth and success, Longs Drug Stores currently operates 381 stores in California, Nevada, Colorado, Hawaii, Washington, and Oregon, and has more than 18,500 employees. Currently, Longs records annual sales of approximately $3.3 billion nationwide.

GROWING UP IN NORTHERN CALIFORNIA

When a new Longs drugstore opens, Petrucelli, like his predecessors, has one focus in mind: "to be the best drugstore in town." This commitment was inspired by the founders of Longs Drug Stores, brothers Joseph and Thomas Long.

The company's history dates back to the late 1800s and the Long brothers' great-grandfather, Goodwin Scudamore, co-owner of three drugstores. Scudamore's successful enterprise paved the way for his son, Thomas E. Long, to open the family's first merchandise store in 1902 in Covelo, California. Shortly after the store's opening, Long died and left the store to his son, Edward.

In 1932, after receiving college degrees, Edward's sons, Joseph

and Thomas, decided to join their family's entrepreneurial heritage. The two young men approached the president of Safeway Grocery Stores, M.B. Skaggs, for a loan, and in 1938, the brothers opened the first Longs Self-Service Drugs. By 1940, the Long brothers had opened two more stores in northern California. The first Central Valley location opened in the heart of downtown Fresno on May 25, 1942.

GROWING STRONG WITH THE COMMUNITY

By 1948, the Longs chain was operating six stores in California, and continued growing through the 1950s and 1960s at a fast pace, adding 31 stores throughout the state. In 1971, Longs was listed on the New York Stock Exchange, and the firm continued to expand, adding more merchandise to each store and priding itself on the utmost in quality products and service.

Today, Longs professional pharmacies are complemented by a broad assortment of merchandise specially chosen by each store manager. The pharmacies assure people-oriented customer service and technology-oriented efficiency. Furthermore, each Longs store prides itself on service in the community, and participates in activities such as health screenings, vaccinations, flu shots, and fund-raising activities for causes that include the Juvenile Diabetes Foundation and City of Hope. The company is also partnered with the Red Cross for disaster relief.

"We believe our original focus on quality customer service and the attention to our employees, vendors, and community are the reasons why our customers consider Longs the 'best drugstore in town,' " says Petrucelli. "We will always work with these main goals in mind, and that is why we continue to grow."

LONGS DRUG STORES HAS SPENT MORE THAN 60 YEARS AT THE TOP OF THE NATION'S DRUGSTORE CHAIN INDUSTRY, AND IS MOVING STRONGLY INTO THE 21ST CENTURY WITH A RICH HISTORY BUILT ON TRADITIONAL VALUES.

LONGS IS CONTINUING TO GROW, RECENTLY OPENING STORES IN FIG GARDEN (RIGHT) AND ON THE CORNER OF CLINTON AND BRAWLEY IN FRESNO.

Fresno Pacific University

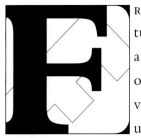

FRESNO PACIFIC UNIVERSITY HAS BECOME AN EDUCATIONAL INSTI-tution that shares its vision with the community, combining faith and knowledge to produce leaders measured by their service to others and dedication to their community. "Fresno Pacific University, while offering the same excellence in education as other universities, is an alternative," says Allen Carden, Fresno Pacific University president. "What makes us special is that we look at the entire student. Beyond the education, we also address the spiritual side."

MOSAIC OF CULTURES

Founded in 1944 as the Pacific Bible Institute, the school started with seven staff members and 28 students. Since then, the university has grown to more than 200 faculty and staff serving 1,600 students on its 42-acre campus located in central Fresno.

Initially, the students and faculty shared the ethnic and denominational heritage of the Mennonite Brethren Church. But as the San Joaquin Valley took on a broader range of cultures and religions, so did Fresno Pacific University. The university today exists to prepare students for thoughtful and wise service through excellence in higher education, and to strengthen faith through scholarship.

Fresno Pacific University is the only accredited, private, four-year Christian university of liberal arts and sciences in central California. The university offers bachelor of arts degrees in five academic divisions, featuring a long list of majors.

At Fresno Pacific University, students may also receive a master of arts degree in education, administrative leadership, and conflict resolution. The university's dedication and commitment to higher education is taken very seriously, which is evidenced by the fact that its graduates are accepted into law, medicine, business, and other graduate programs at Harvard, Yale, USC, UCLA, and the University of Notre Dame.

In Fresno Pacific graduate school, programs are geared to meet the needs of professionals as well as recent college graduates, and are structured to blend both theory and practice. It is with this important blend, and the combination of spirituality and self-growth, that Fresno Pacific University strives to prepare all students for leadership in every community, educational institution, business firm, and civic and nonprofit organization.

Fresno Pacific University also cultivates skills to make learning a lifelong endeavor, offering courses by mail and over the Internet to more than 12,000 educators and other professionals through the Fresno Pacific School of Professional Studies, founded in 1970. For working adults who have not had the chance to complete their higher education, Fresno Pacific University opened the Center for Degree Completion in 1990.

"Fresno Pacific University is a true believer in the idea of lifelong education," says Carden. "We will continuously work to offer

FRESNO PACIFIC UNIVERSITY HAS BECOME AN EDUCATIONAL INSTI-TUTION THAT SHARES ITS VISION WITH THE COMMUNITY, COMBIN-ING FAITH AND KNOWLEDGE TO PRODUCE LEADERS MEASURED BY THEIR SERVICE TO OTHERS AND DEDICATION TO THEIR COMMUNITY.

the opportunity to learn—both academically and spiritually—to everyone we can."

BEYOND THE BASICS

To further promote academics, the university boasts a student/faculty ratio of 15-to-1 and an average class size of 16. All freshmen and sophomores are matched with faculty members and a group of peers to make their integration into studying and social activities easier.

The Older Adult Social Services Program was created in 1981 to stress the need to be involved in and care for the communities near Fresno Pacific University. Continuing to address the needs of people in the surrounding areas and throughout the community, the university organized the Center for Peacemaking and Conflict Studies in 1990. The center helps students recognize that, using their faith, they can help find peaceful ways to resolve conflicts.

EXTRACURRICULAR ACTIVITIES

Since the university and faculty are committed to helping students develop in all aspects of their lives, participation in such student organizations as the Associated Students of Fresno Pacific University and the Student Executive Council is encouraged.

Promoting healthy competition, Fresno Pacific University is a member of the Golden State Athletic Conference, an integral part of the National Association of Intercollegiate Athletics. The university is proud of the Sunbird athletic teams, which compete at the intercollegiate level in men's basketball, cross-country, soccer, and track, and women's basketball, cross-country, track, and volleyball.

The university's theater department produces a variety of full-length stage productions, readers theater, and one-act plays, and hosts a traveling drama group. The music program offers a variety of musical classes, as well as the concert choir, which takes a major tour each year.

Watching over each student, the faculty and staff at Fresno Pacific University help to counsel and provide a family atmosphere for those leaving home for the first time. Fresno Pacific University offers on-campus living and assists students in locating off-campus living. The university offers unique off-campus education by being part of a consortium that features national and international settings for education. Study abroad programs are available, and an American Studies program is offered in Washington, D.C.

Fresno Pacific University embraces diverse cultures and faiths,

preparing students to reach their full potential by providing a full range of academic, cultural, and public service programs. Students grow while furthering their aspirations and embracing their community on a daily basis. The students at Fresno Pacific University today are the community leaders of tomorrow.

Fresno Yosemite International Airport

CONNECTING TRAVELERS WITH FAMILY, FRIENDS, BUSINESS opportunities, and vacation spots, the Fresno Yosemite International Airport continues to evolve into a state-of-the-art facility with a new look for a new century. ■ Originally a military base, the airport was transferred to the ownership of the City of Fresno in 1946. The airport was named the Fresno Air Terminal, with the designator FAT. Renamed Fresno Yosemite International Airport in 1996, the facility is easily accessible from the highways and freeways that transverse the Central San Joaquin Valley.

Situated on 2,150 acres, the airport has two parallel runways that are oriented on a northwest-southeast axis. The principal runway is 9,222 feet long and can accommodate any type of aircraft in service today. The second runway, 7,206 feet long, is used primarily by smaller commercial and commuter aircraft. The instrument landing system for the largest runway is being upgraded to Category II/ILS. When completed in 2000, it will alleviate many winter fog delays.

UPGRADING WITH THE TIMES

A state-of-the-art airport is vital to the economic growth of the region. Our goal is to develop into the regional airport of choice for the 1.2 million people living in the Central San Joaquin Valley," says Charles R. Hayes, director of transportation for the Fresno Yosemite International Airport. The concourse was remodeled in 1998. The 45,000-square-foot terminal building contains ticket counters, baggage-handling areas, and other passenger services. A major addition to the concourse will begin in March 2000 and will be completed in December 2001. The two-story concourse will house a food court, a business center, and passenger boarding bridges that afford immediate aircraft access.

More than 1 million people fly in and out Fresno Yosemite International Airport annually. Seven airlines operate 74 daily departures with more than 2,500 seats nonstop to cities including Dallas, Las Vegas, Los Angeles, Phoenix, Salt Lake City, San Diego, San Francisco, and Seattle. Jet service

CARGO, PASSENGER, AND MILITARY AIRCRAFT OPERATE WITHIN SIGHT OF THE MAJESTIC SIERRA NEVADA AT FRESNO YOSEMITE INTERNATIONAL AIRPORT.

MORE THAN A MILLION PASSENGERS USE FRESNO YOSEMITE INTERNATIONAL AIRPORT ANNUALLY.

continues to grow with 15 jet departures daily. Under the deregulated environment of the airline industry, the airport administration continuously analyzes passenger flight data and community growth patterns to promote expanded air service and recruit new carriers to better serve the residents of the region.

MORE THAN COMMERCIAL AVIATION

The Fresno Yosemite International Airport is home to the California Air National Guard, California Highway Patrol, California Army National Guard, and U.S. Marine Corps Reserve. During the fire season, the U.S. Forest Service and the Department of Forestry operate an air attack base to fight forest fires with their aerial tankers. The airport is home to many cargo carriers, including FedEx, ABX, DHL, and UPS, which generate an estimated $250 million in revenue for the local economy.

More than 200 corporate and privately owned aircraft are based at the airport. Many are high-performance business jets and multiengine aircraft. Three major fixed-base operators—Corporate Aircraft, Central California Aviation, and Mercury Air Center—offer a wide range of services,

including aircraft sales, fueling service, repairs, maintenance, aircraft hangar storage, tie-down facilities, air taxi and charter, and flight instruction.

SERVING THE COMMUNITY

In addition to the renovations to the terminal and concourse buildings, Fresno Yosemite International Airport is continually working to create a safe environment both on the ground and in the air. The airport will upgrade its entryway, moving the airport's entrance to the corner of McKinley and Peach avenues, and will double the amount of parking. The terminal frontage will be renovated to permit easier passenger drop-

off and pickup. The entire cost of the project is approximately $40 million. No tax dollars will be spent on the improvements. The project will be financed through airport revenues and the proceeds of airport bonds.

Along with its goal to modernize air operations, the airport has also set a goal to better educate the public about aviation. In 1998, the airport initiated a program to educate grade-school children in flight travel. "Many of these children have never been on an airplane or to an airport," says Patti Miller, spokeswoman for the airport. "And parents who accompany the tours are gratified to see the changes taking place at Fresno Yosemite International Airport."

SCHOOL TOURS OFFER VALLEY STUDENTS AN OPPORTUNITY TO EXPLORE THE MANY FACETS OF AVIATION.

Valley Children's Hospital

VALLEY CHILDREN'S HOSPITAL BEGAN SERVING THE CHILDREN of the San Joaquin Valley on November 12, 1952, with 42 licensed beds and a medical staff of 118. Specializing in pediatric health care, Valley Children's remains the first and only facility of its kind in central California. ■ The idea of a children's hospital began with five young women: Carolyn Peck, Patty Randall, Gail Goodwin, Agnes Crockett, and Helen Maupin Ross. Concerned with their own children's health care, they began a fund-raising and community involvement campaign in 1948. With the help of the newly formed Valley Children's Guilds, more than $1 million was raised and created a legacy of caring that has grown for more than 50 years.

Over the years, Valley Children's Hospital has added clinics and services from Modesto to Bakersfield—where a new cardiology clinic has just opened—and from Bishop to the coast. Today, it serves children in 10 California counties covering a 60,000-square-mile area.

On September 22, 1995, the board of trustees broke ground on a new facility overlooking the San Joaquin River. The first patients were moved from Shields and Millbrook, and admitted into the state-of-the-art hospital on October 31, 1998. There are currently 242 licensed beds at Valley Children's Hospital.

The new hospital is designed to be child-friendly. A patient advisory team helped architects create a bright, colorful environment where children can feel comfortable. A five-year-old child can see over the counters, and the sterile atmosphere of adult hospitals is absent. Children can enjoy private rooms with sleeping accommodations for their parents, private baths, and sliding panels to hide intimidating medical equipment.

The new facility also features many technological and medical advances, such as the new G.E. short-bore magnetic resonance imaging unit (MRI). This machine is smaller and less intimidating to children, and collects images much faster than older models. Another high-tech diagnostic modality is the new digital Cardiac Catheter-

ization Laboratory, also one of the most advanced in the country.

Valley Children's Hospital physicians practice in more than 36 subspecialties covering nearly every aspect of advanced pediatric care. The hospital features the highest-level neonatal intensive care and pediatric intensive care units in the world, as well as the only pediatric trauma receiving center between Los Angeles and San Francisco. Surgeons specialize in everything from general pediatric surgery to neurosurgery. There are wings devoted to hematology/oncology, rehabilitation, pulmonology, and cardiology. The hospital also houses outpatient clinics with services ranging from diabetes to genetics.

In addition, the hospital owns and operates neonatal intensive care units in Hanford and Merced, California. Other partnerships and clinics are spread throughout the San Joaquin Valley. In Fresno, there are three Pediatrics Plus urgent care centers and a mobile asthma clinic van, which travels to schools to offer asthma screening and on-site care.

At Valley Children's Hospital, physicians, administrators, and staff realize children are not just small adults—they require special care to meet both their physical and their emotional needs. The mission of the hospital is to provide high-quality, cost-effective health care to all children and their families through visionary leadership, exemplary service, and partnerships with other organizations and health care providers.

GEORGE THE GIRAFFE WELCOMES VISITORS TO VALLEY CHILDREN'S HOSPITAL (TOP).

AT VALLEY CHILDREN'S HOSPITAL, PHYSICIANS, ADMINISTRATORS, AND STAFF REALIZE CHILDREN REQUIRE SPECIAL CARE TO MEET BOTH THEIR PHYSICAL AND THEIR EMOTIONAL NEEDS.

THE NAME THOMCO INSURANCE ASSOCIATES, INC. WAS CREATED in 1989, and comes from an appropriate combination of the last names of the firm's founders, Blayne Thomas and Jim Coleman. They have merged their knowledge of the insurance industry and their people-oriented work ethic into a successful business for their employees and customers throughout

the San Joaquin Valley and the state.

"Our staff strives to provide the best possible coverage, and we are committed to giving our customers the most conscientious personal service and economical cost," says Coleman. "We take pride in this approach, and are known throughout the valley for it."

WORKING AND GROWING TOGETHER

Thomas, the founder and original owner of Blayne Thomas Insurance, and Coleman, the current owner and president of ThomCo, have watched the agency grow in both production and personnel. Licensed in California, Oregon, Washington, Idaho, Arizona, Utah, and Nevada, the agency is a member of Group 500, a network of insurance brokers stretching throughout the United States and Canada, working to ensure all details in a customer's insurance plan.

ThomCo has a highly trained staff to handle insurance coverage for its home, business, auto, life and health, and workers' compensation plans. ThomCo also special-

izes in coverage for the trucking, farming, swim school, flower grower, and service station industries. The agency works with many large accounts, including the American Transfer Co. and Zip Trucking, and covers many small-business accounts, including one-day special events.

"If we don't have someone in our office who specializes in the particular needs of a customer, with our network of people, especially the Group 500, we can find someone to help them," says Coleman.

A TEAM EFFORT

Starting with an office in Clovis, California, ThomCo moved to its own building in Fresno, which now serves as the home office for all five of the agency's branches. The Fresno office oversees all the accounting and cash transactions for the five other branches, which include offices in Goleta, Shaver Lake, Paso Robles, Delano, and Redding, California.

With sales reaching more than $10 million in 1999, the agency has shown steady growth for each

year of service. What was once a two-agent office has expanded to employ four commercial customer service representatives, three personal lines customer service representatives, an office manager, an accounting manager, two accounting assistants, and a full-time receptionist in the Fresno office alone.

The agency is fully automated in commercial lines, personal lines, and accounting procedures for the insurance industry. The staff is trained to utilize the latest in computer software for insurance and is now working in a paperless environment.

Coleman enjoys the team aspect of his business and, as the president and admitted coach, believes in setting and reaching goals. "We are a team and a family," he says, noting that his two sons are also involved in the business. "Working together as a family, keeping up with the technology, being aggressive, and personalizing our service are important to us, and we are committed to excellence. I think this transfers across to our customers, and that is our main goal."

"OUR STAFF STRIVES TO PROVIDE THE BEST POSSIBLE COVERAGE, AND WE ARE COMMITTED TO GIVING OUR CUSTOMERS THE MOST CONSCIENTIOUS PERSONAL SERVICE AND ECONOMICAL COST," SAYS JIM COLEMAN, FOUNDER OF THOMCO INSURANCE ASSOCIATES, INC.

KJEO Channel 47

KJEO Channel 47, the CBS affiliate in Fresno, first went on the air the evening of September 31, 1953. Broadcasting from its new studio on Shaw Avenue near the Fresno State College campus, the event featured a dedication ceremony attended by Governor Earl Warren, clergymen, educators, politicians, and other dignitaries from Fresno.

After the ceremony, a 30-minute national show, *You Asked For It*, was broadcast, followed by an adaption of William Saroyan's play *The Time of Your Life*. The station then signed off for the evening. Station president J.E. O'Neill, whose initials form the call letters of the station, announced that starting the next day, the station would operate daily from 3 p.m. to midnight.

More than 45 years later, KJEO Channel 47, now a part of Seattle-based Fisher Broadcasting, continues to serve the communities of the Central San Joaquin Valley with award-winning news and entertainment. "We're very serious about our motto, '47 On Your Side,'" says General Manager Don Drilling. "Our station

J.E. O'Neill founded KJEO Channel 47 in 1953 on Shaw Avenue.

cares about the San Joaquin Valley, and the professionals here at KJEO take pride in looking out for their community."

OUTSTANDING COVERAGE

The dedicated and talented KJEO news team strives for only the best in its newscasts. The team has won numerous awards for its efforts, including, most recently, the Edward R. Murrow Award in 1999 for "Secret War, The Hmong Journey to a New World;" the Radio-Television News Directors Association's 1999 Best Specialty Reporting award for "Scam Busters;" the Fresno County Farm Bureau's award in 1999 for "Vanishing Harvest;" the Emmy Award in 1998 for best light-news series for *Smoking—Kick It;* the Fresno County Farm Bureau's 1998 best news coverage award for "Water of Life;" the Tulare County Teachers award in 1998-1999 for best media coverage for "Earlimart Flooding;" and the 1997-1998 California Coalition for Childhood Immunization award for best TV coverage statewide.

"Although awards are a nice way to be reminded that you're on the right track, the real

reward is the day-to-day life in the streets, finding the stories and telling them in the most compelling way possible," says News Director Alex McGehee.

GIVING BACK TO THE COMMUNITY

O'Neill first founded KJEO to give something back to the people of the San Joaquin Valley. As a local-area farmer and rancher who had immigrated to Fresno from his native Canada with $17.50 in his pocket, O'Neill believed his television station would help improve the standard of living in the area. That concept still drives the KJEO staff, which is as dedicated as ever to the valley.

"We take our public responsibility very seriously, and continually seek new opportunities to reach out to the community," says Drilling. "A television station is a public institution, and civic pride and commitment go along with that."

To this end, management and staff coordinated annual fundraisers to help pay for helicopter purchases for the Fresno Police Department. KJEO's VIP (Very Inspirational Person) program gives attention to citizens in the community who have a positive influence.

216   FRESNO

The news team tackles tough issues with specials such as "Vanishing Harvest," "Urban Sprawl," and "Juvenile Boot Camp." And more than $20,000 was donated to the Make-A-Wish Foundation in 1999 through the station's annual Tournament of Dreams.

STATE-OF-THE-ART DELIVERY

Just as in 1953, KJEO relies on modern technology to improve and expand its service. The KJEO Web site is an efficient and valuable tool for both the viewer and the station. Visitors to the site may view numerous up-to-the-minute, reader-friendly articles in a multitude of categories, including breaking news, important local issues, weather, sports, entertainment, shopping, living, and health. A special feedback section lets browsers register their opinions and chat with others about specific issues of the day. Visitors can also find updated programming schedules and links to information on their favorite CBS prime-time shows.

Many more exciting changes in the television industry are on the horizon, the most important of which is the advent of digital television. Digital television, which will deliver a crisp, clear picture and CD-quality sound, promises to revolutionize the telecommunications industry, and KJEO will be at the forefront of this broadcast revolution in the San Joaquin Valley. KJEO is already making preparations

to broadcast in this new format.

With a dedication to the community and a commitment to the latest in technology, KJEO has become a leader in the

Fresno-area television market. Keeping its founder's vision in mind, the station will continue to achieve success for decades to come.

JUST AS IN 1953, KJEO RELIES ON MODERN TECHNOLOGY TO IMPROVE AND EXPAND ITS SERVICE.

Gunner & Andros Investments

ESTABLISHING ITSELF AS MORE THAN JUST A BUILDER AND developer, Gunner & Andros Investments has a unique and thoughtful way of doing business that set an early pattern of success for partners Richard Gunner and George Andros. ■ Beginning their partnership in 1969 with the construction of a 17,000-square-foot office building in Fresno, the partners

acted as owner-contractors, and were able to achieve considerable savings with new building construction and property improvements. Gunner and Andros also function as their own leasing agents, a position that gives the firm a thorough understanding of the marketplace and the added benefit of familiarity with a tenant's needs.

Property management functions are also performed in-house at the firm. "One of the strengths of Gunner & Andros—beyond our relationship as partners—is that we know this community inside and out," says Andros. "We know the market and we know how to deliver our expertise in management to our clients."

One goal underscores the work accomplished at Gunner & Andros: Each building constructed is regarded as a long-term investment, not a turnaround sell-off for a quick profit. The partners have sold off very few of the buildings they have built over the last three decades, and now manage more than 700,000 square feet of the firm's office space in Fresno.

GUNNER & ANDROS INVESTMENTS HAS SOLD OFF VERY FEW OF THE BUILDINGS IT HAS BUILT OVER THE LAST THREE DECADES, AND NOW MANAGES MORE THAN 700,000 SQUARE FEET OF THE FIRM'S OFFICE SPACE IN FRESNO (TOP).

FRESNO'S DOWNTOWN REVITALIZATION EFFORT IS PART OF A PROPOSAL BEFORE THE REDEVELOPMENT AGENCY OF THE CITY OF FRESNO TO DEVELOP 30 ACRES NEAR THE CONVENTION CENTER, A LONG-TERM INVESTMENT THAT WILL REQUIRE MORE THAN A DECADE TO COMPLETE (BOTTOM).

◄ H.S. BARSOM PHOTOGRAPHY

TENANT SATISFACTION

One of the benefits to Gunner & Andros' strategy of retaining the company's real estate holdings is a high retention of tenants. It is this intelligent approach to property management that has kept scores of the same tenants in Gunner & Andros properties since the 1970s, and it is not unusual for many tenants to expand their space or relocate to another Gunner & Andros complex.

"We always listen to our tenants. We've known from the beginning that people don't come back if they're not pleased," says

Gunner. "We've had many tenants stay with us for decades, and we look forward to working with them in the new century." Tenants range from small, local companies to Fresno's largest legal firms to national corporations. Prospective tenants will find a wide variety of Gunner & Andros business properties, from garden-style office complexes to multistory, Class A office buildings.

DOWNTOWN REVITALIZATION

Gunner & Andros has always succeeded with hard work and old-fashioned values. Both raised in Fresno, Gunner and Andros look forward to the future of the community with a revitalized downtown area. The revitalization effort is part of a proposal before the Redevelopment Agency of the City of Fresno to develop 30 acres near the convention center, a long-term investment that will require more than a decade to complete. The company hopes this long-term vision and commitment to downtown Fresno will serve as a foundation for others to follow.

Providing quality construction and intelligent, efficient administration of its properties, Gunner & Andros Investments maintains a solid reputation as a builder and property management company with a commitment to tenants and to the long-range goals of Fresno.

◄ AC MARTIN PARTNERS

FRESNO

1970	BOYLE ENGINEERING CORPORATION
1970	FASHION FAIR MALL
1972	MANCO ABBOTT, INC.
1972	UPRIGHT, INC.
1973	ALLIANT UNIVERSITY
1973	GRUNDFOS PUMPS CORPORATION
1978	GUARDIAN INDUSTRIES CORPORATION
1980	INTERNATIONAL ENGLISH INSTITUTE
1980	SUNRISE MEDICAL/QUICKIE DESIGNS
1980	WILLEY TILE COMPANY
1981	ECONOMIC DEVELOPMENT CORPORATION
1981	PAYROLL PEOPLE INC.
1981	SAN MAR PROPERTIES INC.

Boyle Engineering Corporation

ESTABLISHED IN 1942, BOYLE ENGINEERING CORPORATION OPENED its Fresno office in 1970. Almost immediately, the office became a force on the local scene, thanks to its high-quality engineering designs and expert consultations. The firm provides a full range of services in civil, electrical, mechanical, and structural engineering; environmental investigations and remediations;

instrumentation and control systems; and transportation. The scope of Boyle's work covers everything from planning through construction management for both public sector and private industry clients worldwide.

"Because Boyle is a strong, employee-owned company, we are able to work on a wide variety of projects," says Keith T. Campbell, managing engineer of the Fresno office. "In addition, our professional and support staff in the various regional offices know the areas in which they work—both geographically and in terms of technical specialty." Campbell is one of many engineers in the Fresno office who graduated from the engineering program at California State University-Fresno.

Boyle's Fresno office often works closely with staff members in the Sacramento and Bakersfield offices. Companywide, more than 80 percent of Boyle's business comes from repeat clients, who take comfort in knowing their projects are in good hands. The firm annually ranks as one of

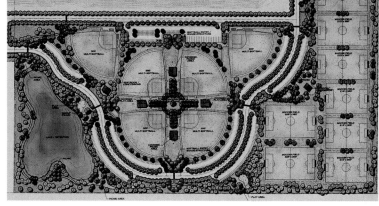

the top 100 pure design firms in *Engineering News-Record* magazine's list of the top 500 design firms.

THE EARLY YEARS

J.R. "Lester" Boyle founded Boyle Engineering in 1942. In 1945, he formed a partnership with Harold Patterson, and the two set out to help private and public agencies solve water problems. Patterson moved on in 1948, and the business became a sole proprietorship—J.R. Lester Boyle, Consulting Engineer.

By 1952, the business was so successful that Boyle incorporated

the company as Boyle Engineering, and a growing staff began addressing the problems associated with a population surge in Orange County, California. The newly incorporated firm formed an alliance among the expansive Metropolitan Water District of Southern California, the Municipal Water District of Orange County, and 20 surrounding water districts. Boyle helped the coalition build major water pipelines to serve Orange County's large population. The firm also developed plans for sewer systems for two sanitation districts.

Boyle didn't pass up opportunities to broaden the client base and expand its services, either. For instance, the firm developed a lasting relationship with the U.S. Department of Defense, which relied on Boyle's expertise to help design civil infrastructure for military installations such as the Trident submarine base in Kings Bay, Georgia.

In the 1970s, Boyle established itself as a nationwide firm. Shortly after opening offices in Bakersfield and Fresno, the firm ventured into Nevada and Arizona. Boyle, who served as president until 1971 and as chairman until 1973, provided the impetus for nationwide expansion, and Thomas S. Maddock, who succeeded Boyle as president, encouraged the corporation's growth. Today, Boyle maintains

NOW UNDER CONSTRUCTION, THE FRESNO LANDFILL REGIONAL SPORTS PARK IS A PROJECT WITH TWO MAJOR BENEFITS: IT WILL LEAD TO THE FINAL CLOSURE OF A LAND-FILL AND PROVIDE NUMEROUS RECREATIONAL OPPORTUNITIES.

BOYLE ENGINEERING CORPORATION HAS DESIGNED MORE THAN 20 WELL-HEAD TREATMENT FACILITIES FOR THE CITY OF FRESNO. MOST INVOLVE THE USE OF GRANULAR ACTIVATED CARBON (GAC) VESSELS IN WHICH GROUNDWATER CONTAMINANTS ARE ADSORBED AND REMOVED BY CARBON.

offices in Arizona, California, Colorado, Florida, Nevada, New Mexico, Texas, and Utah. Maddock is now chairman of the board, and Daniel W. Boyd is president and CEO. Both have been with the company for more than 25 years.

KNOWLEDGE PUT TO GOOD USE

Almost half of Boyle's 500-person staff hold professional registrations in engineering disciplines. The firm has experienced specialists in the areas of land planning, hydrology, water resources, water treatment and wastewater reuse, transportation, electronics, physical chemistry, cost engineering, computer sciences, and automated mapping/facilities management.

Clients of the Fresno office benefit from five specialty groups: agricultural irrigation, computer services, engineering services, traffic/transportation, and water resources. Through these specialty groups, Fresno team members solve the problems that confront both rural and urban areas.

One of the biggest ongoing projects for the Fresno office has been wellhead treatment. In the last decade, the staff has developed plans and specifications for more than 20 new wellhead treatment facilities in Fresno, putting city wells back into production after contamination from a banned pesticide known as DBCP. Also, Boyle specialists have designed experimental sprinkler systems, subsurface drip systems, and other techniques to help farmers reduce water use and produce less drainage water.

Two of the more exciting projects that the Fresno office is working on are a regional sports park and an intelligent transportation system (ITS). Teaming with the landscape-architecture firm The Beals Group, and working from a conceptual layout produced by the City of Fresno's parks staff, Boyle engineers have produced plans and specifications for the Fresno Landfill Regional Sports Park project, which will turn a soil-borrow area for a closed landfill into a first-rate park. When construction of the

park wraps up, the facility will boast two championship soccer fields, six standard soccer fields, six softball diamonds, several play and picnic areas, a pavilion for weddings and receptions, and a lake.

The ITS that Boyle is designing will eventually synchronize hundreds of traffic signals in downtown Fresno. Having recently completed phase one of the ITS, the Boyle team is now in the process of designing a traffic-operations center that will serve as a major component of the ITS. Much of the funding for this project comes from the Intermodal Surface Transportation Efficiency Act's congestion management and air quality program. "The ITS project will make it possible to improve traffic flow and help prevent motorists from getting

held up by a succession of red lights," says Campbell.

The Fresno office of Boyle doesn't confine its work to within city boundaries, but instead provides professional services for clients throughout the San Joaquin Valley. From the women's state prison in Madera to the Main Street Bridge in Porterville, the results of Boyle's work are evident in many locales in central California.

"The staff members in Fresno consider ourselves fortunate because we can rely on the resources of a national corporation to provide the best expertise and services to our local clients," says Campbell. "We have some of the brightest professionals in the industry, and everyone is committed to doing the best job possible to serve our clients in the beautiful San Joaquin Valley."

BOYLE IS A NATIONWIDE FIRM WITH PROJECTS FROM COAST TO COAST. A SIZABLE PERCENTAGE OF THE FIRM'S WORK IS IN TRANSPORTATION, INCLUDING LIGHT-RAIL COMMUTER SYSTEMS LIKE THE MISSION VALLEY WEST LINE IN SAN DIEGO (TOP).

BOYLE PROVIDES A WIDE RANGE OF CIVIL ENGINEERING SERVICES. THE BREADTH OF THE FIRM'S CAPABILITIES IS A MAJOR REASON WHY BOYLE IS A POPULAR CHOICE FOR CORRECTIONAL FACILITY PROJECTS IN THE SAN JOAQUIN VALLEY (BOTTOM).

Fashion Fair Mall

ESTABLISHED IN 1970 AS THE FIRST PREMIER INDOOR SHOPPING mall in the Central San Joaquin Valley, Fashion Fair Mall continues to set the standard for excellence in retail shopping. Hundreds of thousands of customers yearly visit the mall, which is set on 68 acres of land in the heart of central Fresno, to browse the shops and choose from the countless products and services available. With more than 120 stores and a strategic location only one block east of Freeway 41 on Shaw Avenue, Fashion Fair Mall is also host to four major department stores: Macy's, Macy's Men's & Children's, Gottschalks, and JCPenney.

"We are truly a one-stop shopping mall," says Karla Davis, marketing director. "We have three banks; seven unique, multicultural eateries in our food court area; and a wide variety of stores to accommodate our customers." In addition, Fashion Fair houses several retail merchandise units, known as carts, that feature a number of different items ranging from designer sunglasses to cellular phones.

Fashion Fair's 874,306 square feet of space also includes financial services; food and candy shops; women's, men's, and family apparel and shoe stores; housewares stores; jewelry, gift, and card shops; and bookstores. In addition to the food court, the mall has other fast-food facilities and restaurants that serve great burgers, tasty Chinese dinners, and many other delicious meals.

Consumers will find the latest in fashion at The Gap, Express, Victoria's Secret, Wilson's Suede and Leather, and Miller's Outpost, to name just a few of the popular clothing stores. There is something for everyone, from the finest in fashions to best-selling books to toys for children.

Today, Fashion Fair still holds the title for being one of the San Joaquin Valley's finest indoor shopping centers. In a beautiful atmosphere with opaque skylights, large planter pots filled with healthy trees and colorful flowers, and monitored climate control during the warm days of summer, patrons can stroll through the mall and delight in the latest high-tech gadgets for sale, or they can rest with a coffee while people-watching or window-shopping. Always immaculately decorated for the holidays, the mall attracts a multitude of diverse customers who return each year for the fantastic selection of goods and services, as well as the friendly reception they receive from the merchants.

A CHANGE OF SCENERY

Built by the G.L. McDonald Corporation, Fashion Fair was initially a reflection of Fresno's growth and popularity, with people traveling from as far away as Bakersfield and Sacramento to shop. Fashion Fair is now owned by Macerich, a real estate investment

ESTABLISHED IN 1970 AS THE FIRST PREMIER INDOOR SHOPPING MALL IN THE CENTRAL SAN JOAQUIN VALLEY, FASHION FAIR MALL STILL HOLDS THE TITLE FOR BEING ONE OF THE SAN JOAQUIN VALLEY'S FINEST INDOOR SHOPPING CENTERS.

trust. The company is one of the nation's largest owner-operators of regional malls, and is publicly traded on the New York Stock Exchange. Since its inception, Macerich has earned a formidable reputation by purchasing regional malls and transforming them into outstanding retail centers through reconstruction, leasing, specialty leasing, strong management, and marketing expertise. Currently, Fashion Fair has 31 employees who make sure all mall customers' needs are met.

Open 362 days a year, Fashion Fair offers a safe environment with state-of-the-art surveillance equipment and a security force to escort customers to their cars, assist in battery jumps, unlock cars, provide wheelchairs and strollers, and generally ensure shoppers' safety.

MAKING GOOD THINGS HAPPEN

Macerich dedicates itself to reinventing retail businesses, constantly trying to improve on its mixture of tenant locations to enhance consumers' shopping experiences. For example, to make the shopping experience as enjoyable as possible, Fashion Fair offers the Shop-&-Save Club, a loyalty-based incentive program that provides extraordinary customer service, adding those extra touches that make a big difference.

"The club membership is free," says Davis, "and whether it's a safety pin you need, a local phone call, free photo copies and faxes, or a diaper just in case—if it is something customers need, we'll help them find it; that's how we do things. As our mission says, We Make Good Things Happen."

Working to make good things happen is a mission that extends beyond the boundaries of Fashion Fair for Macerich and its employees, as well as the merchants and their staffs. Annually, Fashion Fair will participate in more than 50 events—including flower shows, art exhibits, and children's poster displays—for service clubs, charitable organizations, schools, and special events.

Macerich's ongoing objective with Fashion Fair is to create an exciting environment for consumers, while contributing to the surrounding communities. "It means a lot to us at Macerich and the mall to have events that support and entertain the community," says Davis. "We make sure Fashion Fair is truly a place to have the ultimate shopping experience. We'll continue to grow and look ahead—whether it's renovations or something new—always putting the customer's experience as our first priority."

FASHION FAIR'S 874,306 SQUARE FEET OF SPACE INCLUDES FINANCIAL SERVICES; FOOD AND CANDY SHOPS; WOMEN'S, MEN'S, AND FAMILY APPAREL AND SHOE STORES; HOUSEWARES STORES; JEWELRY, GIFT, AND CARD SHOPS; AND BOOKSTORES (TOP).

WITH MORE THAN 120 STORES AND A STRATEGIC LOCATION ONLY ONE BLOCK EAST OF FREEWAY 41 ON SHAW AVENUE, FASHION FAIR MALL IS ALSO HOST TO FOUR MAJOR DEPARTMENT STORES: MACY'S, MACY'S MEN'S & CHILDREN'S, GOTTSCHALKS, AND JCPENNEY.

Manco Abbott, Inc.

ANCO ABBOTT, INC. HAS ENDEAVORED TO MAKE CENTRAL CALIFORNIA a better place to live while it conducts business as the area's largest and most established property management firm. In its growth and through its employees, the company has exhibited both a caring attitude and the highest level of professionalism. ■ Established in 1972 as Manco West, Manco Abbott's headquarters is located in

Fresno with branch offices in Bakersfield, Stockton, and Carmel. The firm manages shopping centers, apartments, industrial complexes, and office buildings. It handles day-to-day operation of the properties, provides high-quality maintenance supervision, monitors the market to optimize rent levels, and consults with owners on methods to increase income.

But Manco Abbott delivers more than just the standard in its problem-solving support for its properties. For example, the firm provides monthly reports, statistical information, and comparative studies on property operations. The reports detail an analysis of each month's operation results, income and expense levels, and budget variances. These key indicators focus on the progress of each investment as measured against the individualized management plan.

As a result of this eye for detail, Manco Abbott counts as clients such firms as Ralph's Grocery Co., Bank of America, Lend Lease, Wells Fargo Bank, Wilson Development, ICI Development, Koll Investment Management, Betty Galante, Leeds & Strauss, and many others. Manco Abbott is noted for its outstanding personal service regardless of the size of the real estate investment managed.

TOP-NOTCH LEADERSHIP

Manco Abbott's two principals bring varied yet complementary talents to the table. Hal Kissler, certified property manager (CPM), chief executive officer, and the company's original founder, is a graduate of California State University-Fresno. With an extensive background in investment counseling, business, and real estate management, he is a past president of the local chapter of the Institute of Real Estate Management (IREM), and his affection for the Fresno area has made an imprint on Manco Abbott's business philosophy.

Michael S. Goldfarb, CPM and chief operating officer, has decades of experience at the highest corporate levels in property management. He is a past president of Security Management, one of the country's largest property management companies, and has served as president of Florida's largest multifamily housing developer. He is a past president of the Fresno IREM chapter and past director of the California Apartment Association-Fresno.

Both Kissler and Goldfarb have received the Man of the Year award from the San Joaquin chapter of IREM. Their management skills have kept Manco Abbott on track during its steady growth.

Manco Abbott has gathered a top-flight group of professionals to round out the executive management team. Maureen Spenhoff, chief financial officer, has been with Manco Abbott for more than 17 years; Gloria Schermerhorn,

ESTABLISHED IN 1972, MANCO ABBOTT, INC. CONDUCTS BUSINESS AS THE AREA'S LARGEST AND MOST ESTABLISHED PROPERTY MANAGEMENT FIRM, WITH HEADQUARTERS LOCATED IN FRESNO AND BRANCH OFFICES IN BAKERSFIELD, STOCKTON, AND CARMEL (TOP).

IN ITS GROWTH AND THROUGH ITS EMPLOYEES, MANCO ABBOTT HAS EXHIBITED BOTH A CARING ATTITUDE AND THE HIGHEST LEVEL OF PROFESSIONALISM (BOTTOM).

ROBERT A. EPLETT

ROBERT A. EPLETT

ROBERT A. EPLETT

ROBERT A. EPLETT

executive vice president, and Judy Russell, human resources, have both been with the company for more than 20 years. This management team is supported by highly qualified technical personnel in such areas as engineering, supervision, accounting, data processing, and legal affairs.

SUCCESS IN PROPERTY MANAGEMENT

What best demonstrates Manco Abbott's success is the impact its projects make on the community. While taking over the management of a Tehachapi apartment complex that was drug infested, run down, and bankrupt, the firm's creativity, expertise, and hard work turned things around. The occupancy rate rose from less than 20 percent to more than 80 percent, and the bank was able to sell the property for its intended asking price—all in a relatively short span of time.

Manco Abbott achieved results of a similar nature when it took

ROBERT A. EPLETT

over management of one of the largest apartment complexes in Fresno. The property had fallen into foreclosure and was more than 25 percent vacant. Once again, Manco Abbott brought the occupancy rate up to more than 96 percent. What had been a problem property sold for more than $18 million.

While these turnarounds demonstrate the firm's ability to perform for its clients, they also create a marked improvement in the quality of life for the community. Manco Abbott took properties that were contributing to neighborhood neglect and crime, and made them whole again, improving living conditions for the entire area.

CONTRIBUTING TO THE COMMUNITY

Manco Abbott's civic involvement goes beyond improving neighborhoods; Kissler is committed to giving back to the community. One of the firm's major community projects is the Marjaree Mason Thrift Store. Every Manco Abbott employee is asked to work in the store a minimum of four hours per week on company time. Their service, which varies from folding clothes to management duties, has helped transform the thrift shop from a financial drain to a moneymaker. It now generates revenue that helps the Marjaree Mason Center with the various needs of its domestic violence shelter's occupants.

Through its business dealings and its work in the community, Manco Abbott strives to increase the value of its clients' assets and the value of life in the community. Manco Abbott is dedicated to making Fresno a better place to live and to demonstrating that property management is more than just managing property.

CLOCKWISE FROM TOP LEFT: MICHAEL S. GOLDFARB, CERTIFIED PROPERTY MANAGER (CPM) AND CHIEF OPERATING OFFICER, HAS DECADES OF EXPERIENCE AT THE HIGHEST CORPORATE LEVELS IN PROPERTY MANAGEMENT.

LE PROVENCE IS ONE OF THE NEWEST CONDOMINIUM RENTALS IN FRESNO.

HAL KISSLER, CPM, CHIEF EXECUTIVE OFFICER, AND THE COMPANY'S ORIGINAL FOUNDER, HAS AN EXTENSIVE BACKGROUND IN INVESTMENT COUNSELING, BUSINESS, AND REAL ESTATE MANAGEMENT.

GUARANTEE TOWERS IS ONE OF SEVERAL COMMERCIAL PROPERTIES UNDER THE MANAGEMENT OF MANCO ABBOTT.

ROBERT A. EPLETT

UpRight, Inc.

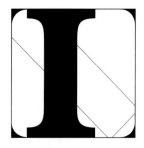

IN 1947, WALLACE JOHNSON STARTED UPRIGHT SCAFFOLDS WITH the invention of an aluminum scaffolding system with adjustable legs to help him paint his hillside home in Berkeley, California. Changing the way people look at heights and how to adapt to them to complete a job, Johnson's creation captured the essence of the post–World War II engineering spirit, the

need for new ideas and new structures, and the growing interest in high-rise buildings.

Johnson next used his talents to develop an innovative commercial grape harvester. The invention was a success and, needing more space to meet the demands for the harvester, UpRight expanded to Fresno County by opening a factory in Selma in 1972. A few years later, Johnson introduced the Flying Carpet, the first of many very successful aerial work platforms.

Today, the UpRight brand of boom lifts and scissor lifts is well known worldwide on construction sites and in maintenance applications at industrial plants and commercial buildings. In 1980, UpRight became a public company, but returned to private ownership in 1987, and has remained that way ever since. During this same time, the company moved its Berkeley operations to officially set up headquarters in Selma. UpRight sold its interest in the grape har-

vester manufacturing business in 1989, and set out to become one of the largest aerial work platform manufacturers in the world.

A FOCUSED PRODUCT LINE

UpRight today offers a diverse product line distributed through a large dealer network across the globe. UpRight produces self-propelled boom lifts and scissor lifts; portable personnel lifts used in schools, hospitals, and universities; aluminum scaffolding systems; and telescopic material handlers, which are commonly used in construction to lift thousands of pounds of materials to overhead work sites.

The company's products have been used in various ways, from aluminum scaffolding used to help restore the Sistine Chapel, to satellite construction work with NASA. In Fresno, UpRight's articulated and telescopic boom lifts have been used regularly at the new Valley Children's Hospital and in the restoration of the city's Historic Water Tower downtown.

UpRight continues to pursue Johnson's innovative spirit, recently debuting the SB80 telescopic boom lift. Weighing 32,500 pounds, the unit is capable of lifting 600 pounds in workers and materials to a maximum height of 86 feet. The SB80 is designed to maneuver well in muddy, wet, or sandy conditions and uneven terrain often found at construction sites.

DEDICATED TO QUALITY

A leading manufacturer in its industry, the company has experienced record sales and found a successful marketplace around the world. "We produce a quality machine, and we pride ourselves on being a company that is easy to do business with," says Barris

THE UPRIGHT, INC. SB80 BOOM LIFT IS USED TO INSPECT THE RECENTLY RESTORED FRESNO WATER TOWER.

Evulich, vice president and general manager at UpRight. "Our customers know we fully support the products we sell, from the day they are manufactured until the last day of their service life." UpRight is dedicated to the safety of its clients and devotes considerable financial resources to the research and development of its products.

GIVING BACK TO THE COMMUNITY

With its new marketing plan in action, an increase in product demand, and a desire to keep its competitive edge, UpRight opened a second San Joaquin Valley plant in Madera, California, in 1998. The plant, which manufactures boom lifts and telescopic handlers, has grown to more than 300,000 square feet of manufacturing and office space.

UpRight's administration and employees are proud of the new Madera factory, which includes a new training center (UpRight University) with 4,320 square feet of classroom and administrative space. "UpRight is excited about the training center," says Evulich. "It gives us a chance to help educate and employ more people in the community. UpRight also offers training to existing employees to help with advancement goals."

UpRight celebrates the new century with revenues in excess of $200 million, and employs more than 900 people in California

alone. "Even though we are a multinational company, we look at what we can do for the community and the region," says Evulich.

"UpRight will continue to move in this direction and to build the best machines available for our customers and dealers."

MAXIMUM WORK SPACE FOR PERSONNEL, TOOLS, AND MATERIALS IS ASSURED WITH UpRight's LX41 SCISSOR LIFT.

UpRight's WORLD HEADQUARTERS IS LOCATED IN SELMA, CALIFORNIA.

Alliant University

ALLIANT UNIVERSITY, FORMERLY KNOWN AS THE CALIFORNIA School of Professional Psychology (CSPP), opened in 1969 as the nation's first independent graduate school of professional psychology. With a campus in Fresno, a satellite location in Sacramento, and three other campuses throughout California, Alliant University offers a range of master's and doctoral level programs, including programs in psychology, management, social and policy studies, education, and other related human service fields.

Alliant University will continue the long-standing CSPP tradition of blending professionalism and science into a training program designed to meet the changing needs of society. For a quarter-century, Alliant University has been training students to work in a broad range of mental health, forensic, and business fields, including hospitals, community health services, and the juvenile and adult justice sys-tems. "We cover many areas of study, with a particular emphasis on practice careers, applied research, and addressing community prob-lems," says Chancellor Mary Beth Kenkel, Ph.D.

THE FRESNO CAMPUS

Alliant University established its Fresno school in 1973, offering the Central Valley's first and only doctoral program. Over the years, programs were added in organizational behavior, for-ensic and school psychology, and community development. The administration and faculty work to meet the many needs of the students, studying the diverse demographic changes that have occurred in the population both on and off campus. "We have many adult learners," Kenkel says. "And we see a number of full-time workers who are chang-ing careers." To meet the stu-dents' needs, Alliant University is adapting programs to offer more options for part-time and distance education.

ADAPTING AND WORKING WITH THE COMMUNITY

Alliant University is com-mitted to its students and to the community, adhering to a continuing philosophy that the completion of the graduate pro-gram is a joint responsibility. Alliant University's fully accred-ited educational programs train individuals who will be able to respond effectively to individual, family, organizational, school, and community problems and needs. Alliant University gradu-ates and students provide a major portion of the mental health ser-vices in the San Joaquin Valley today. Increasingly, some of the Valley's brightest and most suc-cessful managers are being trained by Alliant University.

At Alliant University's W. Gary Cannon Psychological Services Center, faculty and stu-dents are involved in community outreach and service delivery. Their work furthers the school's mission of improving the lives of people within Fresno commu-nities. The center offers general psychological services and pro-grams targeted to people with special mental health needs. The center works with local govern-mental agencies, school districts, justice systems, and other non-profit agencies to ensure the best mental health care for the people of Fresno.

FOR A QUARTER-CENTURY, ALLIANT UNIVERSITY HAS BEEN TRAINING STUDENTS TO WORK IN A BROAD RANGE OF MENTAL HEALTH FIELDS, INCLUDING HOSPITALS, COMMU-NITY HEALTH SERVICES, AND THE JUVENILE AND ADULT JUSTICE SYS-TEMS (TOP).

ALLIANT UNIVERSITY, FORMERLY KNOWN AS THE CALIFORNIA SCHOOL OF PROFESSIONAL PSYCHOLOGY, OPENED IN 1969 AS THE NATION'S FIRST INDEPENDENT GRADUATE SCHOOL OF PSYCHOLOGY (BOTTOM).

ORKING OUT OF THE BASEMENT OF HIS HOME IN BJERRINGBRO, Denmark, Poul Due Jensen started a company, Grundfos Pumps Corporation, that is now recognized as the world's leader in pump technology. In 1946, the young man built his first pump, and within one year, regular production had begun. In 1961, the company—initially called the Bjerringbro Foundry and Machine

Factory—began exporting its products to the United States.

In 1968, the company received its present name, created with the Danish words "grund foss," which mean "ground spring." With approximately 95 percent of the profits reinvested into the company, Grundfos has expanded its economic base and developed the Grundfos Group worldwide. The Grundfos Group is represented by 53 companies in 36 countries, employing more than 9,550 people internationally. Each company of the Grundfos Group is locally managed and operated.

Grundfos Pumps (USA), part of the Grundfos Group, has its sales and manufacturing headquarters in Fresno and its eastern regional headquarters in Allentown, Pennsylvania. Grundfos USA employs 350 locally in positions ranging from customer service to engineering, Internet development, production, warehousing, and after-sales service. The firm offers one of the best combinations of wages and benefits found in any manufacturing company in the Fresno area.

"Our collective vision is to have a highly effective organization that operates in a team environment that values honesty, openness, and involvement from all employees, and fosters cooperation by empowering each person to perform their roles in an environment of trust," says Sam Geil, vice president in Fresno. "From this, we believe all good things—such as profits, sales, market share, and highly motivated people—will come."

QUALITY PRODUCTION

Grundfos Pumps Corporation has an annual production of 10 million submersible and centrifugal pump units. The company offers a wide variety of pumps for commercial/industrial,

plumbing/HVAC, water supply, wastewater, and environmental applications. Registered to the ISO 9001 international quality standard since 1993, Grundfos is committed to the continuous improvement of the quality of its products and services. In further recognition of its quality efforts, Grundfos recently received an Achievement Award conferred by the California Governor's Quality Awards Program. Grundfos also holds ISO 14001 registration for environmentally sound business practices.

Known for its expertise in the fabrication of stainless steel, a technology Grundfos helped pioneer, the company has now added cutting-edge electronic expertise to its extensive list of product features. In 1992, Grundfos introduced pumps featuring an embedded microchip to automatically sense and adjust pump performance. This variable speed technology has been developed further to include features such as remote control operation and data collection. Grundfos' continuing research and development efforts secure the company's reputation as Leaders in Pump Technology.

"Our people, and our ability to create innovative products,

maintain our leadership in the market," says Geil. "There isn't a pump company in the world that produces as many new and innovative products as Grundfos."

Grundfos USA will further its organization's goals by exploiting technology, continuously developing its people, and cultivating business-to-business relationships with its distribution partners. "Our goal for the future is to continue to build a healthy organization that is team-focused," says Geil. "This means consensus management, high employee involvement, continuous improvement, and a learning organization that appreciates innovation, exploration, mistakes, and continuous personal and professional growth."

GRUNDFOS PUMPS CORPORATION IS HEADQUARTERED IN FRESNO (TOP).

GRUNDFOS PUMPS CORPORATION OFFERS A WIDE VARIETY OF PUMPS FOR COMMERCIAL/INDUSTRIAL, PLUMBING/HVAC, WATER SUPPLY, WASTEWATER, AND ENVIRONMENTAL APPLICATIONS (BOTTOM).

Guardian Industries Corporation

THOUGH IT HAD A MODEST BEGINNING IN 1932 IN DETROIT AS a windshield fabricator for automobiles, Guardian Industries Corporation has become the third-largest flat glass manufacturer in the world. The privately owned company—headquartered in Auburn Hills, Michigan—now operates in 15 countries on five continents and serves millions of customers.

"At Guardian Industries, our philosophy is that a company, like people, should grow each year in vision, in performance, and in accomplishment," says William Davidson, who has been president of the company since 1957. Davidson's winning philosophy has empowered his more than 15,000 employees to produce float glass and fabricated glass products for construction and automotive applications.

Guardian Industries broadened its original product line, beginning with flat glass manufacturing in 1970—and subsequently opened a plant in Carleton, Michigan. This was the first time the floating glass process had been introduced into a primary glass business in the United States in 50 years.

The floating glass process involves floating molten glass made from sand on a bath of molten tin to produce a ribbon of nearly perfect glass with high optical clarity. Similar to the mixture of water and oil, the tin's density separates it from the floating molten glass in this unique formative process.

Although today Guardian Industries markets many products, the company is best known for its architectural glass for the commercial and residential markets. With its knowledgeable use of technology and resources Guardian Industries also produces a broad range of fiberglass insulation. Every Guardian Industries product is manufactured according to strict safety and environmental regulations.

LOCAL AND GLOBAL OPERATIONS

Located just minutes south of Fresno, Guardian Industries currently operates San Joaquin Valley's Kingsburg plant, which was opened in 1978. The company also operates another plant in Reedley, which functions as a distribution center, as well as a production plant for mirror glass used in homes and a wide range of construction projects. In addition, Guardian has new plants now operating in New York and West Virginia.

The company has made great strides over the last three decades, adding 19 new float lines throughout the world. In addition, it has acquired more than 20 glass fabrication plants. Guardian Industries entered the global market in western Europe in 1981. Opening a plant in Luxembourg furthered its European expansion by branching out into Spain, Hungary, and Germany. Today, operations are thriving globally, as proven by plants in Venezuela, Thailand, and India, and by glass distribution centers in Brazil, Japan, Argentina, and South Africa.

Many of the world's most prominent skylines are enhanced with Guardian Industries glass, which can also be found in interior and exterior applications for the home. The company stands behind its products, and it works hard to meet both the technical building requirements and the environmental needs of each project. As a result, Guardian Industries Corporation continues to succeed in sales and expand its new plants and products.

GUARDIAN INDUSTRIES CORPORA-TION IS TODAY THE THIRD-LARGEST FLAT GLASS MANUFACTURER IN THE WORLD.

AFTER ATTENDING THE AMERICAN UNIVERSITY IN CAIRO IN THE 1970s, Anne Speake, owner and president of International English Institute (IEI), saw a need for a family-oriented environment where people from across the globe could come to share their cultures, ideas, and experiences while learning English. From her travels as a student, Speake knew what it was

like to blend and adapt into a new culture while trying to absorb the language. She returned to Fresno to open IEI in 1980 with 17 students and four employees.

IEI has since grown into one of the most prestigious English language institutes in the world. It has served as host to more than 30,000 students and professionals from 70 countries over the last 20 years, helping people to learn or enhance their knowledge of the English language. "The institute embraces culture as well as the language," says Speake. "We consider ourselves not just teachers, but also those who promote international friendship and cultural understanding."

THE FINEST FACULTY AND CURRICULUM

IEI has a highly trained faculty, with the majority holding advanced degrees in English as a Second Language. The staff—which includes Speake and her daughter, Lisa—is dedicated to providing the finest quality education, and works to emphasize the similarities between their students, not the cultural differences. In 1990, IEI was honored to receive the U.S. Small Business Administration's Business of the Year in California award.

Approximately 1,000 people enroll at IEI every year, and students are able to choose from a variety of programs. IEI offers four programs on a year-round basis to students who want to learn English, travelers who would like to learn as well as see the local sites, and professionals looking to expand their English skills. These programs include the Intensive English Program, College English Preparation Program, Holiday Homestay English Program, and the English for Specific Purposes Program.

IEI's Homestay Director works with 250 Fresno-area families to help introduce American culture

to nonnative speakers of English for both academic and professional purposes. "Our Homestay Program is very popular, and it's something I'm very proud of," says Speake.

The homestay families who open their homes are rigorously screened. The housing director interviews and monitors the families and the students, and then completes a thorough evaluation at the end of each student's stay.

NOT JUST A CAMPUS ATMOSPHERE

The IEI campus is built around a beautiful courtyard, with spacious classrooms, an administrative center, and an activity center specially designed for students. The institute is committed to creating a comfortable family environment for students, and often offers excursions to Yosemite National Park, San Francisco, and the Pacific Ocean.

IEI also has a state-of-the-art Sony digital audio lab, and offers

students the latest in technology with a multimedia computer lab featuring IBM-compatible systems and access to the Internet.

Not only do students achieve a comprehension of the English language and cultural understanding, they also enrich the Fresno community, bringing in both diversity and approximately $5 million annually in revenue. "We work to bring people together," says Speake. "We are proud of the goodwill people share through international friendships."

INTERNATIONAL ENGLISH INSTI-
TUTE HAS GROWN TO BECOME ONE
OF THE MOST PRESTIGIOUS ENGLISH
LANGUAGE INSTITUTES IN THE
WORLD.

Willey Tile Company

ARMED WITH TALENT, RESOURCES, AND AN ENDLESS APPETITE for the challenges that lie ahead, Willey Tile Company has excelled in providing quality products and uncompromised craftsmanship to its customers. President and CEO Larry Willey and his family credit their strong work ethic, quality of service, and dedication to the community for the company's current success. After achieving recognition as an officer for the Madera County Sheriff's Department's Narcotics Enforcement Division, Larry Willey decided to try something new. Having learned tile installation from his father-in-law, Willey opened the one-man shop in 1980 that has become the San Joaquin Valley's largest tile company. "I've always believed that true success can be seen in how much you give back and help people," Willey says. "That goal is equal to the job we do for our customers. It has to be 100 percent all around."

Willey has built his company on the values he learned as a child. In his 16-hour workday, he accomplishes tasks ranging from designing tile work for a family in their new or remodeled home to assisting one of the many service clubs, nonprofit organizations, or political entities he volunteers for daily.

CUSTOMER CARE AND SERVICE

Inside Willey Tile Company's 10,000-square-foot warehouse, customers will find the latest in tile selections and materi-

als including glass block, porcelain, granite, mini brick, limestone, marble, and slate. "As styles change, we'll add to our stock," says Willey. "We always keep up on the latest trends in tile selection, and I enjoy consulting on design projects. The trend now and for the near future is toward larger tiles, and there are always new colors, shades, and patterns to consider." With more than 20 years of design experience, Willey has gained a reputation as an innovative designer with his use of color and pattern. Willey Tile

Company completes more than 1,500 jobs annually, varying from work in custom and tract homes to apartment complexes and businesses from Modesto to Bakersfield. The company also specializes in stone installation and fabrication, marble-edge finishing, and insurance cases, as well as remodeling and commercial work. Project goals are met by the highly skilled, 60-member staff, comprised of a full-time crew of estimators, a warranty division, a warehouse staff, and installation experts. Because customer satisfaction is first and foremost, Willey insists on offering the best warranty service available, as well as an easily accessible warranty department that prides itself on prompt and dependable service.

THE DRIVING FORCE

Whether he is traveling with the mayor to the east coast to promote Fresno, or working closer to home on a design project or a worthy cause, the day starts in the office at 6 a.m. and the agenda is a long one for Willey. Starting off the new century as the chairman of the board of the Fresno Chamber of Commerce, Willey is looking forward to continuing to

WILLEY TILE COMPANY'S INSTALLATIONS MAKE ROOMS LOOK UNIQUE.

INSIDE WILLEY TILE COMPANY'S 10,000-SQUARE-FOOT WAREHOUSE, CUSTOMERS WILL FIND THE LATEST IN TILE SELECTIONS AND MATERIALS INCLUDING GLASS BLOCK, PORCELAIN, GRANITE, MINI BRICK, LIMESTONE, MARBLE, AND SLATE.

spread the news about what Fresno and the San Joaquin Valley have to offer.

"Fresno is just beginning to realize its potential. It is a wonderful city that hasn't been tapped all the way yet," says Willey. "We are so lucky to live in one of the finest cities in the country." According to Willey, the area's low cost of living, diversity, potential for growth, climate, and educational system are all strong incentives to live and do business in Fresno, and not just for Willey Tile Company.

Willey views the company's success as an opportunity to build a better community. As representatives of the Fresno business community, Willey Tile Company employees volunteer to tutor high school students. Willey has served on numerous boards, acted as a passionate advocate of local baseball, and formed ArcWork, a work project for the Association for Retarded Citizens, which is dedicated to helping people with special needs join the workforce. For this accomplishment, Willey and his company received a certificate of recognition from the California State Senate.

Through the Fresno Business Council, the YMCA, the Work Force Development Board, and many more organizations, Willey will work on decreasing the unemployment rate locally. "You must give back to the community," says Willey. The Willey family is also working on increasing the number of the company's employees by 30 percent. Willey's leadership is a trait evident in his own family: His son Brent serves as warehouse manager while attending college full time, and his older son Scott serves as vice president and chief operations officer of the company. Willey's son-in-law, Brian Jensen, serves as chief financial officer.

As a highly competitive company, Willey Tile Company is aware of the market, and how to meet a customer's needs. With its dedication to the community, the company will continue to be a part of Fresno's business landscape for years to come.

Economic Development Corporation

THE ECONOMIC DEVELOPMENT CORPORATION (EDC) SERVING Fresno County was established in 1981 as a private, nonprofit economic development organization. Its mission is to foster new job growth, increase investments, diversify the Fresno County economy, and strengthen local services through the attraction of new companies and the expansion and retention of existing companies in base industries.

The EDC—funded by both private and public investors, as well as grants—offers its investors a range of benefits, and provides information to them regarding companies relocating to the area and how they affect the community. In addition, it promotes business partnerships and relationships among its investors, elected officials, and communities.

The EDC serves Fresno County and its 15 incorporated cities of Clovis, Coalinga, Firebaugh, Fowler, Fresno, Huron, Kerman, Kingsburg, Mendota, Orange Cove, Parlier, Reedley, San Joaquin, Sanger, and Selma, as well as the unincorporated areas of Fresno County.

FRESNO COUNTY

Fresno County is the regional hub for business and industry. Centrally located between the San Francisco Bay Area and Los Angeles, the county provides rapid access to the western United States and the Pacific Rim markets, and is becoming recognized worldwide.

"The Central Valley is becoming the preferred region for companies seeking to expand or relocate in California," says Richard Machado, president and CEO of the EDC. "Fresno County offers a unique combination of affordable real estate, abundant labor, and a centralized location."

Machado adds that the market is particularly attractive to call centers and back-office operations that appreciate the area's state-of-the-art fiber-optic infrastructure and diverse labor pool. Light assembly and distribution/warehouse are also well represented, due to the county's low labor and operating costs and its proximity to nearly 50 million consumers.

Fresno County is ranked as the number one agricultural county in the United States; it provides extraordinary opportunities for the expanding value-added food

FRESNO COUNTY IS RANKED AS THE NUMBER ONE AGRICULTURAL COUNTY IN THE UNITED STATES. IT IS ALSO CONVENIENTLY LOCATED TO YOSEMITE NATIONAL PARK.

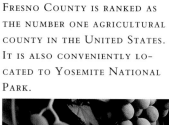

companies. The EDC provides demographic data, which allows targeted companies to maximize the resources available in the county.

"Our job is to provide the most current and state-of-the-art tools available to site consultants worldwide on the benefits of locating in Fresno County," says Machado. "Our labor force is wonderful; the cost of living can't be beat. We're sandwiched between two of the largest metropolitan areas in the nation, San Francisco and Los Angeles, but we're much more affordable. And we are more seismically stable than many areas of the West Coast. Depending upon your industry, that can make a big difference."

LOOKING TO THE FUTURE

The EDC is moving into the 21st century with a strong commitment to the 6,000-square-mile Fresno County region and the motivation to succeed. "I see the business economy of the 21st century to be global, information and knowledge based, fast moving and technology driven, and work-force knowledge dependent," says Machado. "These elements make up the fundamental foundation of the new economy. The EDC will strive to communicate these elements to the business communities to encourage participation in the new economy, which will benefit all the citizens of Fresno County."

processing industry that benefits from its surroundings and strategic shipping location. Other industries thriving in this region include medical, financial, and technological support services.

WORKING FOR FRESNO COUNTY

The EDC recruits companies throughout the world to locate in Fresno County. To accomplish this, the EDC generates interest in the region through the publication of current, factual marketing materials and data; represents Fresno County through marketing missions throughout the United States and internationally; and encourages firms to locate in the region by facilitating their site selection needs in a fair, professional, and confidential manner.

The California Trade and Commerce Agency recognizes the EDC as the lead economic development organization in Fresno County and its partner in eco-

nomic development. The EDC also receives calls directly from prospective companies, and works closely with the local public entities, real estate brokers and developers, and EDC investors to identify and supply information to prospective

Payroll People Inc.

RESPONDING TO A NEED FOR THE OUTSOURCING OF PAYROLL and employer tax pay and file throughout the San Joaquin Valley in the early 1980s, Bettye L. Smith, with Jim Smith and John W. Dodson, founded Payroll People Inc. (PPI), a high-quality business services company. Soon, what had been a regional vision became a national enterprise. ■ Opened in 1981,

PPI has become California's largest independently held payroll company. It now operates with clients throughout the United States, expertly caring for the many non-revenue-producing tasks of thousands of businesses, allowing them to focus their attention on their core missions. "With years of expertise in the payroll industry, PPI handles each client's business as though it were our own," says Smith, president and CEO. "Working with each client's unique needs, delivering complete accuracy and confidence—these are our main priorities."

Smith's many years of commitment to PPI and its clients have earned the company the unique honor of having one of the only women in the industry to hold the distinction of president and CEO. Smith uses her extensive knowledge as a business owner and service provider to help define her industry. In fact, she often travels to Washington, D.C., to appear before U.S. Treasury

officials, representing the payroll industry and her clients by contributing vital information regarding legislation creation and implementation. PPI keeps a close eye on the constant changes in both employment and payroll legislation and legal actions affecting employers' payroll and tax filings.

PPI'S MULTIPLE SERVICES

From the beginning, the company has focused its growth on payroll-related outsourcing services, and Smith has acted as a visionary, driving PPI to build technical systems to develop a line of employer services at the pinnacle of the payroll industry. The company offers clients ranging from small businesses to large corporations a number of services, including payroll processing, payroll tax pay and file management, PC-based client services, automated time accounting systems, employer-related insurance products, employee benefit plans, and human resource software.

Smith has created a dynamic environment for the management of the company. PPI managers maintain a constant focus on meeting clients' goals, offering solutions and services in every area of the businesses' organization. "Our services and our software products are constantly maintained, and they evolve as we forecast industry trends," says Smith. "We are proud to be the sole proprietors of our own software. This way we have the ability to customize system functionalities to meet our clients' specific, and often singular, needs."

PPI's payroll services cover every aspect of an employer's needs, whether handling employee payroll checks or direct deposit; payroll journals; personnel reports; or input by telephone or client-site PC software. The company's comprehensive tax pay and file management service provides a varied array of services, including full compliance with the IRS Electronic Federal Tax Payment

BETTYE L. SMITH IS COFOUNDER AND PRESIDENT OF PAYROLL PEOPLE INC.

System, preparation of tax returns, W-2 processing, response to agencies' inquiries, and guaranteed accuracy of work.

PPI's extended services allow employers to choose control of options from on-site software, multisite reporting, report generation, human resource software, general ledger interface, and automated time accounting systems.

The automated time accounting system collects employee work data to generate tracking reports, integrate employee job data into spreadsheets and databases, generate totals, and estimate wages by user-defined cost centers. The Pay-As-You-Go Insurance program takes care of varying aspects of a company's workers' compensation insurance needs, including premium deductions, and deals with managed care providers offering an optional 24 Hour Insurance program. Benefit services, including administration of 125 and 401(k) plans, provide pretax deductions for insurance, child care, unreimbused medical, and retirement savings options.

DIVERSITY UNDER ONE ROOF

With more than 85 employees, PPI operates three integrated companies under its roof: PPI, Payroll Tax People, and Pay-*e*. Payroll Tax People works to assist businesses, other payroll providers, and financial institutions manage the ever changing arena of employer tax law, technology, compliance,

marketplace demands, and heightened risks. "Accuracy and providing compliance solutions are critical," says Matt Whetton, director of marketing. "We adhere to strict internal regulations that protect our clients from the complicated federal, state, and local payment and reporting rules."

The third division, Pay-*e*, is made up of a team of professionals with extensive experience in the payroll processing industry who have developed and are licensing payroll service bureau software to payroll companies, CPAs, financial institutions, and businesses throughout the nation. Smith is again partnered with Dodson and Jim Smith. All three are instrumental

in Pay-*e*'s software development and are well equipped to forecast the emerging trends in the outsourcing marketplace. Pay-*e*'s biggest asset lies within an in-house group of professionals with an in-depth knowledge of the industry and an experienced team of software engineers.

"We work to achieve a great deal, and we do it successfully and accurately," says Smith. "We have a dynamic team of people who are not just providing a service, but also participating on a community level. We moved into this region to benefit from the quality of life available only here, and have found a wealth of happiness both personally and professionally."

JIM SMITH (LEFT) AND JOHN W. DODSON (RIGHT) ARE COFOUNDERS OF PAYROLL PEOPLE INC.

THE PPI STAFF SUPPORTS A VARIETY OF COMMUNITY-BASED CHARITIES, INCLUDING SPONSORING CASUAL DAY FOR UNITED CEREBRAL PALSY.

SAN MAR
Properties Inc.

ITH MORE THAN 50 YEARS OF EXPERIENCE BETWEEN THEM, Marc A. and Sandra Wilson of SAN MAR Properties Inc. have one goal in mind for their clients: "to manage to make them money." Established in Fresno in 1981, the company has steadily built a reputation as a leader in the San Joaquin Valley. Providing professional real estate management and investment

services, SAN MAR Properties is looking to grow even more in the future and to continue to furnish the best possible return for its clients.

"We take sincere pride in the service we provide," says Marc Wilson, president and CEO of SAN MAR Properties. As a Certified Property Manager® (CPM) and real estate agent, he has a strong history of taking troubled properties and turning them around. "Both Sandra and I believe in hands-on management, in taking care of a property as though it were our own," he says.

GROWTH, SERVICES, AND EXPANSION

SAN MAR Properties actively manages more than 40 apartment communities in California's Central Valley from Bakersfield to Sacramento, including the San Francisco Bay Area. The company

also provides management for single-family homes, condominiums, historic properties, office buildings, and more than 1,300 units through various homeowners' associations.

"We've created a company to which investors can come with either a good situation or a bad one, and we'll use our experience to keep or make that property a success," says Sandra Wilson. "It is wonderful to be able to show a client who has had previous trouble improvements within a month. It makes a difference to them, the residents, and the neighborhood, and that makes us feel good."

SAN MAR Properties was ranked among the industry's top five real estate management firms throughout most of the 1990s by the *Fresno Business Journal*. With more than 105 staff members, including property supervisors, resident managers, rental consult-

ants, maintenance and custodial personnel, and the administrative staff in its corporate headquarters, the company services a varied demographic of clients that include international, national, regional, and local properties.

At SAN MAR Properties, most staff hours go into property management, not into managing the company itself. "We have more supervisors with smaller portfolios than the industry average, and we give more notes and communication to our owners," says Marc Wilson. "We trust our staff and their knowledge, and we know everyone here works with integrity and ethics as their top priorities." Working with customers in the Far East, all over the United States, and throughout the Central San Joaquin Valley, SAN MAR Properties has earned a reputation for its attention to detail and its commitment to its clients' goals

SAN MAR PROPERTIES INC.'S MANAGEMENT TEAM INCLUDES (FROM LEFT) PAT LOCEY, CARL KETTLER, TERRY A. FOX, THERESE EPPS, BARBARA RYLEE, SANDRA WILSON, AND MARC A. WILSON.

SAN MAR PROPERTIES' CORPORATE STAFF HAS EARNED A REPUTATION FOR ITS ATTENTION TO DETAIL AND ITS COMMITMENT TO ITS CLIENTS' GOALS AND OBJECTIVES.

and objectives.

"We're lucky to not have to spend a great deal of time marketing ourselves. Most of our clients come to us as referrals. Our clients are really our marketers," says Sandra Wilson. "We have many clients who have been with us for 12 to 15 years."

A HIGHLY SKILLED TEAM

Designated as an Accredited Management Organization® (AMO) by the Institute of Real Estate Management (IREM), SAN MAR Properties has been honored as part of a select group of management companies that meet the high standards for professionalism required by IREM. With four CPMs on staff, SAN MAR Properties' management team has the expertise to effectively and efficiently manage the firm's extensive portfolio of clients.

With all their success, the Wilsons and their employees take time to give back to the community and their industry. For example, Marc Wilson is a member of East Fresno Rotary, past president of the Apartment Association of Greater Fresno, and past secretary of the executive board of the California

Apartment Association. He is the current president of the San Joaquin chapter of IREM, and was awarded Landlord of the Year for 1990 by the Fresno Rental Housing Association. In addition, he is an instructor at Fresno City College, where he passes along the expertise he has gained through the years, teaching the property management course.

Sandra Wilson is an active volunteer and member of the local chapter of IREM, and has served as president of San Joaquin Chapter Number 85. She serves on the executive board of directors and is a past coordinator for the Accredited Residential Manager training program. In addition, she was honored with the CPM of the Year award for 1991 and 1994.

The Wilsons surround themselves with a winning team of professionals, who make winning plans for their clients. For example, Terry A. Fox, CPM, a licensed real estate agent, earned his bachelor's degree in business administration from the University of Nebraska and his MBA from Boston University. Fox serves as vice president of marketing and business development. He is on the board of directors for the Fresno

Chamber of Commerce and is a former member and treasurer of the Fresno Area Crime Stoppers Program. A graduate of Leadership Fresno, Fox serves on the Leadership Fresno Alumni Association Board of Directors.

Also on SAN MAR Properties' staff is Therese Epps, CPM, who serves as a property supervisor and association division head for the firm. Epps has extensive property management experience and has worked for more than 13 years managing associations in the Fresno area. A licensed real estate agent, she received the Certified Assisted Housing Manager designation in 1993. Epps has served on the board of directors for the Apartment Association of Greater Fresno and is the secretary of the local chapter of IREM.

"We have an understanding of what is going on in Fresno and California in the real estate market, as well as nationally and globally," says Marc Wilson. "We are sincere in our pride for the service we provide, and the result is success from hard work, an aggressive style, a demand for excellence, and, above all, putting the clients' goals first."

Sunrise Medical/ Quickie Designs

THROUGH THE RELENTLESS DETERMINATION AND SPIRIT OF ONE woman, a Fresno-based company has evolved into the cornerstone of an industry, while helping thousands of people worldwide realize their potential. In 1980, Motion Designs, the brainchild company of Marilyn Hamilton and two hang gliding friends, debuted an innovative, customized, lightweight wheelchair called the Quickie. Now proudly owned and operated by Sunrise Medical, Quickie Designs—as the company is now known—still changes the lives of disabled people.

"Our team here in Fresno has the opportunity every day to help people get their lives back and get out there," says Lee Sneller, vice president of manufacturing. "The Quickie is going to be someone's freedom and independence. It's got to be exactly what they want and need."

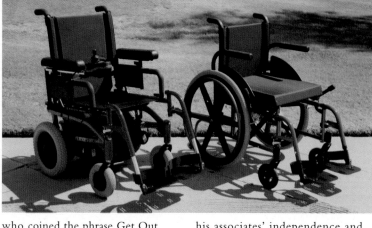

OUT OF NECESSITY

What started out as an invention of necessity for Hamilton, who was paralyzed in a hang gliding accident, soon became a reality. Hamilton quickly realized her new invention could help many people accomplish everyday tasks and tackle the sporting events she longed to be a part of again.

Soon, with the help of her fellow inventors and several sports enthusiasts, production of the wheelchairs began in a 600-square-foot shed, turning out one wheelchair a day. Six years later, the company caught the eye of Sunrise Medical, which bought Motion Designs and kept Hamilton on as a vice president in the marketing department to promote her invention. "It was Marilyn who coined the phrase Get Out There," says Sneller. "She won't take any excuses from herself, and doesn't want anyone else to take excuses either." Hamilton is a six-time disabled ski champion, two-time silver medal Paralympic ski champion, and two-time U.S. Women's Open Wheelchair Tennis champion.

Quickie Designs, now located in eastern Fresno, is one of 13 manufacturing plants belonging to Sunrise Medical—five of which are in Europe—and the only one that produces the lightweight manual and powered wheelchairs. It manufactures the number one lightweight wheelchair in the world.

Sunrise Medical and Quickie Designs fall under the leadership of Michael Hammes, president and CEO. Hammes encourages his associates' independence and awards their innovativeness and compassion, while giving every associate the challenge to live his or her life on and off duty by "doing the right thing."

THE NEED FOR MORE

Growing in popularity each year, Quickie Designs has more than 500 associates on-site who dedicate themselves individually to each chair. Sometimes weighing as little as 18 pounds, the wheelchairs are customized for an exact fit, come in 24 colors, and can be constructed from aluminum, titanium, or steel.

In addition to its adult models, Quickie Designs' team of engineers manufacture the Zippie, a lightweight wheelchair for children ages four and up. The design can be customized to make any client happy regardless of age, and the chairs can grow with the children for more than four years. "All our chairs adapt," says Sneller. "This is why each chair requires many measurements from the client. It must be perfect for them.

"Our main goal will always be to assure quality and motivate people to get out there. They can have the ability to be everything they want to be. We know they can and we'll help make it happen," Sneller says.

FRESNO

Year	
1982	Valley Small Business Development Corporation
1984	Sierra Tel Communications Group
1986	Kaiser Permanente
1986	The San Joaquin Suites Hotel
1986	ValCom Technology Center
1987	Pelco
1991	Kraft Foods–Capri Sun
1994	AT&T
1994	KJWL 99.3
1999	Gap Inc.
1999	The Radisson Hotel & Conference Center

Valley Small Business Development Corporation

STARTING IN 1982 WITH JUST A LOAN GUARANTEE PROGRAM, the Valley Small Business Development Corporation now handles more than a dozen state and federal guarantee and direct loan programs. With a goal of serving businesses that may be overlooked by traditional loan sources, the organization is helping to secure the future for small farms and businesses throughout the valley.

In 1990, the organization began making direct farm loans, guaranteed by the former Farmers Home Administration, now the Farm Services Agency (FSA). Today, Valley Small Business Development Corporation is currently one of only two companies in the state with the expertise to handle both farm and business lending through a contractual arrangement with the State of California. This program came about in December 1990 when Chief Executive Officer Michael E. Foley noticed that some small farmers who had the potential and determination to succeed were being denied loans by banks. He lobbied in Washington, D.C., for the federal government to back up the State of California's farm-loan program, and the effort was successful.

"Rural America has historically had trouble financing new businesses because there is just not enough infrastructure to attract lenders," says Foley. "All you have to do is drive on the west side or the east side of the San Joaquin Valley and try to find a local bank with local lending authority. More often than not, the bank is a branch office that sends loan applications to a regional lending center in a metropolitan area, which may not understand rural issues." Responding to this predicament, the Valley Small Business Development Corporation applied for and won status as an intermediary with the federal government, loaning money to businesses in rural communities with a population of 25,000 or less.

TEAM APPROACH

Foley credits the success of Valley Small Business Development Corporation to a team effort. Consisting of 17 staff members, a volunteer loan committee, and a volunteer board, the team "pulls together and really makes this company work," he says.

The board members, all of whom volunteer their time, realize how important these small-business loans are to rural development. They are all involved in different aspects of rural life, and understand the social and economic issues of small-business and farm loans: Fred Machado of Machado Farms; Judith Soley, attorney at law; Julia Picher, grower and packer; Gordon Saito, certified public accountant; Victor Lopez, mayor of Orange Cove; James Parks, attorney at law; and Timothy Rodriguez, banker, all donate their time to help ensure the Valley Small Business Development Corporation remains successful and these loan programs continue to help small-business owners and farmers.

Another integral part of the loan approval process is the volunteer loan committee. Consisting of members of the local lending community, the loan committee provides a full review of the loan, determines if the loan should be recommended to the board for approval, and—if approval is recommended—makes sure the loan is structured properly. The board of directors has final approval on every loan.

OFFERING A VARIETY OF SERVICES

Farmers with as few as five acres can get financial help from Valley Small Business Development Corporation's Small

THE OWNER OF THIS 65-ACRE ALMOND GROVE WAS THE BENEFICIARY OF A DIRECT FARM LOAN FROM THE VALLEY SMALL BUSINESS DEVELOPMENT CORPORATION.

THE VALLEY SMALL BUSINESS DEVELOPMENT CORPORATION BOARD OF DIRECTORS INCLUDES (STANDING, FROM LEFT) FRED MACHADO, MIKE FOLEY, JIM PARKS, TIM RODRIGUEZ, (SEATED, FROM LEFT) VICTOR LOPEZ, JULIA PICHER, JUDITH L. SOLEY, AND GORDON SAITO.

Farmer Program, a partnership with Wells Fargo and Glendale Federal Bank. Often, small farmers suffer from difficulties in market access and are easily affected by weather disasters, and this program can help when no other financial institution will recognize the opportunity. The organization also administers U.S. Department of Agriculture (USDA) Rural Business Enterprise Grants in the city of Orange Cove; the city of Huron; the Five Cities Economic Development Authority, which includes Reedley, Parlier, Selma, Kingsburg, and Fowler; and along the I-5 corridor. These federal grants are intended to promote small business that will in turn hire or retain employees in rural areas.

In addition to administration of the California Small Business Loan Guarantee program and Farm Service Administration Farm Loan, Valley Small Business Development Corporation handles a variety of other programs, including the USDA Intermediary Relending Program, which promotes small business and employee retention in rural areas; California Disaster Loan Guarantees, which provides fast attention to small businesses and farms hit with disaster; and the Small Business Administration (SBA) Direct Microloan Program, which addresses businesses whose needs are too small for conventional sources. In addition, the organization promotes the California Economic Development Lending Initiative (CEDLI) to provide

market-rate loans to small businesses unable to secure regular funding, as well as the I-5, Orange Cove, and Huron revolving loan fund (RFL) programs, which support small businesses in rural areas. By mid-year 2000, Valley hopes to have met the requirements to become a Certified Development Corporation and begin providing SBA 504 loans for facilities acquisition for small businesses.

Additional Valley Small Business Development Corporation programs include the Central Valley Business Incubator, with loans granted by the University Business Center at California State University-Fresno; SBA Pre-Qualification Loan Program, helpful to businesses with at least 51 percent ownership by women, minorities, veterans, and/ or handicapped individuals; Small Farm/Business Loan Program, providing loans to underserved populations, minority small-

business owners, and farmers; and the California Child Care Guarantee Loan Program, helping licensed child care centers and family day care facilities.

As the largest small-business development corporation in the state, Valley Small Business Development Corporation's loan officers, board members, and staff enjoy an excellent reputation. "When you're dealing with public dollars, you have to be ever vigilant that you treat everyone the same," says Foley.

Over the years, the corporation has made in excess of 990 loans, worth more than $110 million. In 1999, loan guarantee activity generated 1,197 full-time, 92 part-time, and 425 seasonal jobs. For that same period, direct lending created 105 full-time, 46 part-time, and 81 seasonal jobs in the communities served. "We've always maintained the mind-set that we want to get the deal done," says Foley. "We've got some great success stories, and it is very rewarding for our board and staff to see that."

UNDER THE DIRECTION OF FOLEY AND SENIOR LOAN OFFICER LEE TAKIKAWA, VALLEY SMALL BUSINESS DEVELOPMENT CORPORATION WORKS TO SECURE THE FUTURE FOR SMALL FARMS AND BUSINESSES THROUGHOUT THE SAN JOAQUIN VALLEY.

MARY LEONG (LEFT), AGRICULTURE LOAN ASSISTANT, AND DEBBIE RAVEN, VICE PRESIDENT AND SENIOR AGRICULTURE LOAN OFFICER, HELP AREA FARMERS AND RANCHERS SUCCEED (LEFT).

THIS 90-ACRE RAISIN GRAPE FARM WAS FINANCED BY VALLEY SMALL BUSINESS DEVELOPMENT CORPORATION (RIGHT).

Sierra Tel Communications Group

ELPING BUSINESSES FIND THEIR WAY THROUGH THE CONTINUAL advances in the telecommunications world is Sierra Tel Communications Group, a multifaceted corporation offering total communications solutions and exceptional customer service for large and small residential and business customers. ■ With a wealth of experience behind them, Sierra Tel Communications

CLOCKWISE FROM TOP LEFT:
SIERRA TEL INTERNET, A SIERRA TEL COMMUNICATIONS GROUP COMPANY, PROVIDES DIAL-UP INTERNET ACCESS TO A LARGE PART OF THE VALLEY, FROM FRESNO TO KETTLEMAN CITY, AND FROM MADERA TO BAKERSFIELD.

MARCIE SCHWEIKERT IS THE MANAGER OF SIERRA TEL BUSINESS SYSTEMS.

SIERRA TEL COMMUNICATIONS GROUP PRIDES ITSELF ON ITS RURAL ROOTS, AND MOST OF EASTERN MADERA COUNTY RELIES ON SIERRA TEL FOR BOTH RESIDENTIAL AND BUSINESS COMMUNICATIONS NEEDS.

Group subsidiaries—Sierra Tel Business Systems, Sierra Tel Internet, and Sierra Tel Digital Video Network—excel in a variety of business challenges. These companies provide a wide range of products and services, including varying degrees of bandwidth and data transfer, E-commerce Web sites, Internet access, telephone systems, cordless phones, Centrex and voice mail services, pagers and dispatch, personal communications systems, security systems, and video-based solutions. Friendly, skilled technicians; comprehensive customer training; and round-the-clock support are hallmarks of these companies. They provide an impeccable level of service for customers in Fresno, Clovis, and the mountain areas, including Mariposa and Sonora.

"We are a business solutions, people-oriented company," says Marcie Schweikert, manager of Sierra Tel Business Systems. "We will come to your firm and provide consultation, and advise business owners and operators

about current technology and practices, as well as facilitate the infrastructure for a business to get out there and compete in today's high-tech environment."

Sierra Tel also offers a business center at its home office in Oakhurst, complete with copy and fax services, UPS shipping, computer and Internet training, and computer repairs and software. Private videoconferencing is available through the Sierra Tel Digital Video Network division.

Another facet of Sierra Tel Communications Group is Sierra

Tel Internet (STI). STI provides dial-up Internet access to a large part of the Valley, from Fresno to Kettleman City, and from Madera to Bakersfield. STI is continually looking out for its customers with an emergency power facility, capable of keeping the company running 24 hours a day, as well as offering 24-hour free technical support and content filtering. STI continues to grow and will be expanding its services to meet the growing needs of its customers.

AWARD-WINNING SERVICE

Sierra Tel Communications Group prides itself on its rural roots, and most of eastern Madera County relies on Sierra Tel for both residential and business communications needs. Sierra Tel Business Systems' Mariposa satellite office was selected as Business of the Month in September 1999 by the Mariposa Chamber of Commerce. GTE Wireless selected Sierra Tel as its Showcase Business of the Year for 1999. GTE, in its quarterly magazine, *Market Watch*, has also chosen to highlight Sierra Tel for high standards in advertising.

Since its inception, Sierra Tel has built a reputation for being one of Central California's providers of choice for integrated telecommunications solutions and problem solving. As Sierra Tel continues to market total business solutions to the entire Central San Joaquin Valley and beyond, satisfied customers return as their businesses grow. Having earned the reputation of being a well-administered company with quality products and services, well-thought-out plans, and fine-tuned engineering, Sierra Tel Communications Group companies are leading the businesses of the Valley to a profitable, successful future in the 21st century.

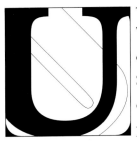

UTILIZING HER TENACITY AND NEVER–SAY-DIE ATTITUDE, VALCOM Technology Center President and CEO Kate Smith has built the company from the ground up. Today, ValCom serves the Central San Joaquin Valley as the leader in its marketplace, providing customers with an efficient and effective combination of computer networks, telephone systems, and videoconferencing.

"I work for everyone here at ValCom, and for every customer who has faith enough to spend a dollar with us," Smith says. Her business philosophy puts all employees on the same playing field, with one goal in mind. "We work as a team, with the customer's satisfaction as our main goal, and we have fun doing it," says Smith. The ValCom team acts as a unit, with staff members participating in the various decision-making processes concerning all aspects of the business.

THE AMERICAN DREAM

Born in the Midwest to a hardworking family, Smith was taught she could do anything she set her mind to. With this conviction, Smith approached the executives at InaCom, Inc. of Omaha with her vision of the future. Offering the company her years of knowledge working in the computer chip and technical industries, Smith received the franchise for Central California.

ValCom opened its doors in 1986 with a three-person team that rapidly grew to more than 50 technical and support personnel who serve more than 5,000 clients. ValCom is able to offer its clients the latest in state-of-the-art technology, including services in all areas of computer networking, Lucent telephone systems, and videoconferencing. The videoconferencing center is Smith's brainchild, available to businesses by appointment and equipped with a high-tech system that connects companies across the globe.

ValCom is located in northwest Fresno in two buildings—one for administration and another for servicing—totaling approximately 13,000 square feet. The fast-growing firm has gained the respect of its clients, many of whom have worked with Smith for more than 20 years. ValCom offers systems configuration services, direct ship programs, total life cycle management services, and a high level of technical support. The ValCom team is highly skilled and has access to resources to keep computer systems up and running, allowing administrators to focus on delivering the best products and services.

GIVING BACK TO THE COMMUNITY

Since its founding, ValCom has received numerous industry awards, including IBM's national Gold Medallion award for the highest level of customer satisfaction, as well as many consecutive Circle of Excellence awards from InaCom. In 1996, Smith received ValCom's highest award for customer satisfaction and quality service.

On a local level, Smith was honored with the Unsung Hero award from the California Association of the Physically Handicapped, and in 1996, the Outstanding Employer of the Year award from the Private Industry Council (now the Fresno Workforce Development Board). "I've been blessed, and there isn't a day when I don't wake up and enjoy coming to ValCom. I work with good people, and together we enjoy expanding our business and the businesses of our clients," Smith says.

KATE SMITH SERVES AS PRESIDENT OF VALCOM TECHNOLOGY CENTER.

Kaiser Permanente

KAISER PERMANENTE, ESTABLISHED MORE THAN 65 YEARS AGO AS the nation's first prepaid health care system, now serves more members than any other provider in California and the San Joaquin Valley. ■ Kaiser Permanente was the vision of Sidney R. Garfield, M.D., who created a group practice prepayment plan for construction workers in the Mojave Desert.

The plan caught the attention of industrialists Edgar and Henry Kaiser, who offered it to their workers, and by 1945, the plan was made available to the public. Kaiser Permanente has evolved into the nation's largest health care system, serving nearly 6 million members in California alone.

Kaiser Permanente is the leader in delivering high-quality care because its unique, integrated system brings together all the elements of health care to successfully meet the needs of members and patients.

Kaiser Permanente is a health care delivery system, not an insurance company. The system's hallmark is the ability to integrate the elements of health care—physicians, hospitals, home health, support functions, and insurance—into a coherent whole.

Kaiser Permanente also is a not-for-profit organization. It has no shareholders and, therefore, its resources are invested in providing affordable, high-quality care for the members and communities it serves.

The doctor-patient relationship, the foundation of Kaiser Permanente's approach to the practice of medicine, is the most important reason the system is unique from other health care organizations. At Kaiser Permanente, all medical decisions are made by physicians in consultation with their patients, not by health plan administrators.

GROWING WITH THE VALLEY

The Kaiser Permanente health care system expanded into the Fresno area of the San Joaquin Valley in 1986 with a commitment to providing members with high-quality, affordable care that emphasizes prevention and a car-

ing relationship with a primary care physician.

Kaiser Permanente Fresno began with a few physicians and 500 members. By 1989, membership had swelled to 42,000 members, and Kaiser Permanente officials announced plans to build a medical center complex at Fresno Street and Alluvial Avenue.

Construction began in 1991, including medical offices, pharmacies, and the optical sales department. Other departments were constructed the following year, and in 1995, the state-of-the-art medical center opened. Recognized with several architectural awards, the nationally accredited hospital is licensed for 121 beds, and features a birthing center where mother, partner, and newborn can stay together throughout the birth process.

EMPHASIS ON PREVENTIVE CARE

Kaiser Permanente Fresno's medical center offers inpatient, emergency, outpatient, prevention, and health education services. InfoTrak, a complete database of health and medical journals, is available to members, and the 24-hour medical advice language assistance program

A SOARING, TWO-STORY GLASS ATRIUM OFFERS A STRIKING AND WELCOMING ENTRANCE FOR KAISER PERMANENTE MEMBERS (LEFT).

KAISER PERMANENTE HAS THREE SITES IN THE SAN JOAQUIN VALLEY, INCLUDING ITS ORIGINAL FACILITY ON FIRST STREET (RIGHT).

◀ JANE LIDZ

includes a Spanish-language service line, as well as a Cantonese and Mandarin line. To fill the need for care in the area's growing communities, Kaiser Permanente also opened a medical office complex in Oakhurst in the foothills northeast of Fresno.

"At Kaiser Permanente, every person involved wants to ensure the best quality in patient care," says Physician-in-Chief Varoujan Altebarmakian, M.D. "We work to keep a patient healthy from the start by emphasizing preventive medicine. Kaiser Permanente physicians work with each member to give them the best care possible."

IMPROVING THE HEALTH OF THE COMMUNITY

Kaiser Permanente is a vital member of the Fresno community, as well as a leading pro-

vider of health care. The organization serves a four-county area including Fresno, Madera, and northern King and Tulare counties. It is the area's sixth-largest employer with more than 125 physicians and approximately 400 registered nurses on staff.

A variety of civic and nonprofit organizations are served through Kaiser Permanente's outreach program, such as the American Cancer Society, Fresno Metropolitan Museum, Marjaree Mason Center, Hispanic Chamber of Commerce, Central Valley AIDS Team, Chicano Youth Center, Sanctuary for Youth, and Stone Soup Fresno.

As part of its commitment to making the lives of children in the area safer and healthier, Kaiser Permanente sponsors a violence prevention program at Fresno's

Pinedale Elementary School. Kaiser Permanente also supports activities in the Fresno, Central, and Clovis unified school districts, as well as districts in Madera, Selma, Kerman, Sanger, West Fresno, and Oakhurst. "Next to our patient care, helping our communities is a top priority," says Altebarmakian.

Kaiser Permanente welcomes the next century by reaffirming its historical commitment to providing quality care to its members and service to its communities. As the country's largest nonprofit health care organization, Kaiser Permanente has earned national recognition for its quality-of-care measures and community service efforts. Kaiser Permanente continues to exemplify the standard for committed, quality care by which all others will be measured.

UTILIZING EMPLOYEE INPUT, THE NURSING STATIONS AT KAISER PERMANENTE FRESNO WERE DESIGNED FOR STAFF EFFICIENCY AND PATIENT SAFETY (LEFT).

KAISER PERMANENTE FRESNO'S NATIONALLY ACCREDITED HOSPITAL IS LICENSED FOR 121 BEDS, AND FEATURES A BIRTHING CENTER WHERE MOTHER, PARTNER, AND NEWBORN CAN STAY TOGETHER THROUGHOUT THE BIRTH PROCESS (RIGHT).

IN 1995, KAISER PERMANENTE FRESNO'S STATE-OF-THE-ART MEDICAL CENTER OPENED, AND HAS SINCE BEEN RECOGNIZED WITH SEVERAL ARCHITECTURAL AWARDS.

The San Joaquin Suites Hotel

HETHER THE OCCASION IS BUSINESS OR PLEASURE, BEING A GUEST of The San Joaquin Suites Hotel is the closest experience to being at home. The hotel opened its doors in the summer of 1986, and Russell Smith, the managing general partner, knew exactly what he wanted to offer his guests: a hotel encompassing a beautiful atmosphere, the latest in luxury and amenities, and unsurpassed service, all in a family environment.

"We really are a one-of-a-kind suite hotel," says General Manager Mary Mendoza, who points out the site was initially an apartment complex before the transformation into a suite hotel. "Having been a nice apartment complex, it was easy for Mr. Smith to create his vision of what he wanted The San Joaquin Suites Hotel to be." Renovations began in 1984 and took two years to complete. In 1995, the hotel completed additional renovations to assure guests the quality they've come to expect.

CREATING THE LUXURY OF HOME

Nestled in the prestigious business and residential neighborhood of Fig Garden, The San Joaquin Suites Hotel fits quietly into the area and greets each guest with a meticulously kept garden, spacious and well-designed hotel suites, and a coastal-like courtyard featuring a pool and spa.

The San Joaquin Suites Hotel now features seven suite designs by Fresno's finest interior decorators. All the suites are indi- vidualized to make visitors feel at home. Guests may choose any suite, from the intimate design of the Squire Suite to the spacious Senator's Suite, with enough room to hold a mini board meeting or just relax with the family when they visit for a weekend getaway to nearby Yosemite National Park.

The hotel is also proud of all its rooms, which include remote televisions with cable, a telephone with a 24-foot cord and computer dataport, a well-lit desk, coffee-makers, and an ironing board. Microwaves are located in both the full kitchens and the micro kitchens. "These are very popular for those who travel often," says Mendoza. "The kitchen is a great luxury. It's these kinds of touches that really make our guests feel right at home."

Many of the suites include a private balcony or patio, and the guests may choose from a one-, two-, or three-bedroom suite, with a living room and bathroom. "The guests are sometimes surprised they can stay in a beautiful suite for the same price they would find at an ordinary hotel," says Mendoza. "We also offer a very nice continental breakfast and a lavish happy hour each day for our guests."

UNSURPASSED SERVICE

Mendoza stresses that it isn't just the beauty of the hotel, the suites, and the courtyard of The San Joaquin Suites Hotel that makes it stand out from its competitors. The service sets it apart as well.

Each guest is greeted by name, and if he or she requires a special publication, a particular kind of pillow, or something from a nearby restaurant beyond the room service menu, Mendoza says the staff will see to whatever is needed. The hotel also has an affiliation

NESTLED IN THE PRESTIGIOUS BUSINESS AND RESIDENTIAL NEIGHBORHOOD OF FIG GARDEN, THE SAN JOAQUIN SUITES HOTEL FITS QUIETLY INTO THE AREA AND GREETS EACH GUEST WITH A METICULOUSLY KEPT GARDEN, SPACIOUS AND WELL-DESIGNED HOTEL SUITES, AND A COASTAL-LIKE COURTYARD FEATURING A POOL AND SPA.

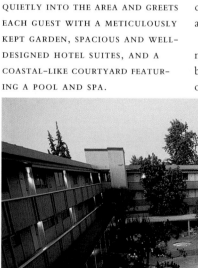

LOCATION IS EVERYTHING

While staying at the hotel, guests can easily access Freeway 41 and Highway 99, parks and recreational areas, an array of fabulous shopping centers, theaters, and the convention center. San Francisco and the Pacific Ocean are just a few hours away, and the Sierra Nevada is even closer.

"Fresno is a great place to be for the hotel; being centralized in the San Joaquin Valley is absolutely perfect," says Mendoza. "Mr. Smith is pleased with how the hotel has turned out and will continue to make his guests the number one priority."

At The San Joaquin Suites Hotel, the owner, management, and staff are constantly looking for ways to improve the property and meet the guests' needs while still keeping the quaintness and elegance that embrace each visitor.

According to Mendoza, many of the clients are corporate guests, but the hotel will often see newlyweds come in for the special honeymoon package. Couples can be dropped off in their limousine, and for no additional cost receive chilled champagne or sparkling apple cider, gourmet sweets, breakfast, and evening hospitality.

If a corporation or wedding party wants to have an intimate reception for their guests, the hotel is equipped to accommodate up to 100 people in the courtyard. With a few days' notice, the staff is happy to help plan the event down to the last detail.

with one of Fresno's finest health clubs, and offers to its guests airport shuttle service; corporate, weekly, or monthly rates; and wedding plans.

THE SAN JOAQUIN SUITES HOTEL'S GUESTS MAY CHOOSE FROM ONE-, TWO-, AND THREE-BEDROOM SUITES THAT INCLUDE CABLE TELEVISION, TELEPHONE WITH DATAPORT, COFFEE-MAKERS, IRONING BOARDS, AND MICROWAVES. THE HOTEL ALSO FEATURES SEVEN SUITE DESIGNS BY FRESNO'S FINEST INTERIOR DECORATORS. ALL THE SUITES ARE INDIVIDUALIZED TO MAKE VISITORS FEEL AT HOME.

Pelco

RESPECTED AS A MAJOR PRODUCT INNOVATOR, PELCO, A privately held, closed-circuit television (CCTV) manufacturer, is a proven world leader in manufacturing high-performance, integrated CCTV security systems. Headquartered in Clovis, California, Pelco not only is one of the largest employers in the Fresno area, but it is also the largest closed-circuit video manufacturing complex in the world.

PROVEN INDUSTRY LEADERSHIP

Although founded in 1957 in Southern California, the company recognizes the beginning of the "new" Pelco as June 1, 1987, when it was acquired by its current owners in Clovis. Prior to that, Pelco's position within the marketplace varied, and it was generally seen as a second-tier player.

The new owners' goal was for Pelco to become the best CCTV supplier in the industry. In order to do that, they realized that first there had to be a huge transformation in the company's corporate culture. A number of programs designed to achieve 100 percent customer satisfaction were imme-

diately implemented, along with employee performance incentives based not on quantity, but on quality.

It took Pelco fewer than two years to turn things around, and the firm has been winning annual top-supplier awards within the security industry ever since. Pelco has also won numerous community and state awards for business excellence, including Employer of the Year in 1998 from the State of California. Most recently, Pelco was honored in the *Congressional Record* as an Exemplary Company for its outstanding service and reputation throughout the Central Valley and across the nation.

Pelco is also a company that gives back to its community. In 1998, during a year when the local Toys for Tots program was being scaled back due to a lack of funding and community support, Pelco employees were credited with almost single-handedly saving the local drive by donating a record-breaking 24,964 toys to the marines. In 1999, Pelco employees donated 73,768 toys, surpassing the program's goal for the entire area.

MARKET EXPANSION AND GROWTH

During Pelco's first 12 years under new ownership, explosive growth added hundreds of new jobs with each facility expansion. Pelco is currently in the process of another expansion, which will increase its workforce to 1,400 after its completion in mid-2000. The company is located in the City of Clovis Industrial Park, where it owns 24 acres and has options on many more. "The City of Clovis has always been marvelous to work with, and we are here to stay," says Pelco President David L. McDonald.

Pelco also has facilities in New York, allowing the firm to compete more effectively on the East Coast. Recently, the company opened additional sales and training offices in Las Vegas and in the Netherlands, as well as a European distribution center.

Beginning with just a few products back in 1987, including

A WIDE RANGE OF PELCO CLOSED-CIRCUIT TELEVISION EQUIPMENT KEEPS A PROTECTIVE EYE ON THE STATUE OF LIBERTY. STAIRWAYS, DOORWAYS, AND MANY OF THE ORIGINAL STATUE COMPONENTS—INCLUDING THE ORIGINAL TORCH ON DISPLAY WITHIN THE STATUE—ARE UNDER VIDEO SURVEILLANCE, IN ADDITION TO THE EXTERIOR OF THE STRUCTURE (TOP).

PELCO IS HEADQUARTERED IN CLOVIS, CALIFORNIA, NEAR FRESNO YOSEMITE INTERNATIONAL AIRPORT. THE STATE-OF-THE-ART FACILITIES WILL TOTAL 400,000 SQUARE FEET IN MID-2000 WHEN THE FIRM'S NEWEST BUILDING IS COMPLETED (BOTTOM).

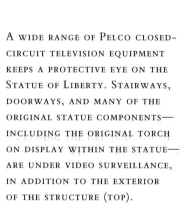

simple pan and tilt positioning units and camera enclosures, Pelco has now grown to offer the most complete CCTV product line in the world. And as Pelco maintains its emphasis on vertical integration while moving toward ISO9000 certification, the firm is very well positioned to meet its next set of challenges in the new millennium.

As the industry continues to redefine itself, Pelco continues to adapt and hold on to its leadership role. The company plans to make many more significant contributions by maintaining a crucial blend of manufacturing, marketing, and engineering strengths.

EXCELLENCE IN CUSTOMER SERVICE

Pelco has an extensive customer base, selling its more than 2,500 finished products through a network of 3,500 dealers throughout the United States and in more than 130 countries. The company's products have been installed in about 300,000 locations worldwide, with the Statue of Liberty being one of the most recent installations.

Pelco realizes that success in business is never a given, but something that must be earned on a daily basis. "The ultimate boss over all of us here is the customer. Nearly everything we do is designed to provide our customers with the most extraordinary level of overall performance possible," says McDonald.

Best known within the CCTV industry for its high level of customer service, Pelco's relentless drive to achieve 100 percent customer satisfaction is as unique today as it was in 1987.

FORMULA FOR SUCCESS — VALUED EMPLOYEES

Generally, when companies look back on their successes, they weigh profits against losses, evaluate market shifts, and ponder the positioning of the company. McDonald acknowledges that a healthy bottom line is what makes Pelco's company culture possible, but he says it's much more than that. Pelco recognizes that people are its most important asset.

Pelco's powerful Surface Mount Technology (SMT) area is capable of producing miniaturized printed circuit boards using advanced digital technology. SMT and the products driven by its capabilities will continue to be a unique, strategic advantage for Pelco (top).

High-end video integration with Pelco's System 9760® allows multiple users to quickly and easily observe multiple camera views for surveillance purposes and provides visual verification when alarms are triggered. Its flexibility addresses the needs and requirements of many different applications, including casino security, transportation, commercial users, and correctional facilities (bottom).

For example, Pelco employees are allowed to do whatever they deem necessary to satisfy customers, without needing approvals from anyone, and by policy, without fear of criticism after the fact. Pelco's three-part formula for successful management obviously works: create an environment that encourages creativity and self-expression, point people in the right direction, and get out of their way.

"The number one motivating factor for individuals, particularly in their work environment, is recognition—more so than job security and even money," says McDonald. Each year Pelco rewards its employees with thousands of company-provided meals and gift items—all relating to achievement and recognition. "People who are recognized, and therefore motivated, are simply better employees who try harder. The end result is an upbeat, winning environment that's fun."

Pelco's past, present, and future success is the result of the contributions of its people, and Pelco's focus on customer service will never lessen, says McDonald. "It's Pelco's culture, our core strength, and the reason we are where we are today."

Kraft Foods-Capri Sun

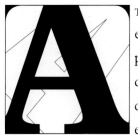

AT THE KRAFT FOODS-CAPRI SUN FACILITY IN SOUTH FRESNO, employees are proud to produce some of the company's most popular refreshments, including Capri Sun All Natural® juice drinks, Tang® soft drinks in pouches, and Kool-Aid Bursts® soft drinks. Kraft Foods purchased the five-acre site in 1991 and has expanded the facility several times to its current, 140,000-square-foot size. Products are shipped from the distribution center in Fresno to customers in 12 western states.

A NEW TASTE AND DESIGN

Capri Sun® juice drinks come in unique flavors such as Pacific Cooler®, Safari Punch®, and Strawberry Kiwi®. Flavors are made from all-natural ingredients and contain 10 percent fruit juice. Kool-Aid Bursts® soft drinks are available in 10 flavors and are sold in six-packs. Both Capri Sun® and Kool-Aid Bursts® drinks are popular with parents and children because they offer ready-to-drink convenience and easy portability that make them ideal for school lunch boxes and travel.

Capri Sun pioneered the single-serve fruit drink design in the United States. The Wild Co. launched the product, which comes in a distinctive foil pouch with a straw, in 1979. The design defined a new age of compact, portable, and disposable containers. In 1985, the Wild Co. bought back the rights to the brand from Shasta Beverages and established Capri Sun, Inc. A manufacturing facility in Fresno was then opened to serve customers on the West Coast.

In 1991, General Foods purchased Capri Sun. General Foods introduced Kool-Aid Bursts® in a plastic squeeze bottle in 1991, and in 1993, began production of this product in Fresno. These two popular brands came into the Kraft Foods product line when Kraft and General Foods merged in 1995.

MAKING EMPLOYEES A KEY TO SUCCESS

The Fresno manufacturing plant and distribution center's aim is to provide high-quality products and services to the grocery industry. Referred to as team members, employees are key to this success through their involvement in the decision-making process at the site. Team members help develop work schedules and starting times that support both business objectives and personal needs. Additionally, each team member is responsible for helping create a personal training program to improve communication and technical skills. Overall, every team member's involvement is part of the high-performance work system approach, which drives business success and greater employee satisfaction at the plant.

Team members are also in-

volved in volunteer activities that support the local community. One key example is the ongoing support for Calwa Elementary School, located near the manufacturing plant, which ranges from financial donations for cultural arts programs to supplying Capri Sun® drinks for school athletic events. Team members have also served as volunteers for the Fresno County Special Olympics, Toys for Tots donation drives, and United Cerebral Palsy fund-raising events.

The Kraft Foods-Capri Sun facility in Fresno is an energized workplace, involving all team members in partnership with their customers, the community, and the environment. The plant continues to thrive and grow in Fresno, and looks forward to many more years in the community.

Kraft Foods, Inc. is the North American food business of Philip Morris Companies Inc. The company traces its rich history to three of the most successful food entrepreneurs of the late 19th and early 20th centuries: J.L. Kraft, Oscar Mayer, and C.W. Post. Today, Kraft Foods is proud to be the largest U.S.-based packaged food company in the world, and works toward continued success, providing quality beverages and food products to millions of people every year.

AT THE KRAFT FOODS-CAPRI SUN FACILITY IN SOUTH FRESNO, EMPLOYEES ARE PROUD TO PRODUCE SOME OF THE COMPANY'S MOST POPULAR REFRESHMENTS, INCLUDING CAPRI SUN ALL NATURAL® JUICE DRINKS (BOTTOM), TANG® SOFT DRINKS IN POUCHES, AND KOOL-AID BURSTS® SOFT DRINKS (TOP).

 ITH A GLOBAL COMMUNICATIONS NETWORK, AT&T ENABLES the world to communicate. In the continental United States, the company's operations handle more than 250 million voice, data, and video calls every day. The company is also busy creating new opportunities for its customers, including wireless and high-speed data, voice, and video communication, as well as digital cable television, which features new and additional premium channels and CD-quality music without commercial interruptions.

COMPREHENSIVE LOCAL SERVICES

Local customers may take full advantage of all the benefits of AT&T's expansive global network and comprehensive business services. The company partners with many Fresno businesses, providing not only high-tech business and communications services, but also its vast experience in successful networking and technical innovations. "At AT&T, we are specialists in business communication and the Internet," says Curt Jones, Wireless Services' general manager of the Fresno office. "We are always looking ahead and incorporating the use of cutting-edge technologies and service."

AT&T offers several packages to local businesses, including a comprehensive service that combines voice, data, advanced features, access, local, long-distance, audio teleconferencing, and wireless services in one commitment. Customers can also choose toll-free, outbound, network management, international, and 900 services.

AT&T Business Solutions goes a step further to provide customers with a complete line of strategic networking solutions, including the AT&T Campus Alliance, Global Network Services, Small Business Center, and AT&T Solutions. In addition, AT&T's Women in Business program offers opportunities for women in business to network with their colleagues.

Local businesses find many advantages in partnering with AT&T, receiving not only high-tech business and communications services, but a company with vast experience in successful networking. And AT&T Laboratories is a pioneering

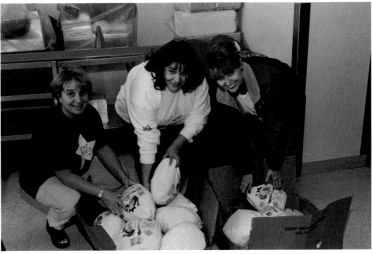

force in the industry, responsible for a variety of communications innovations from computers to cellular telephones.

COMMUNITY CONNECTION

AT&T prides itself on being a good corporate citizen worldwide, as well as in the Central San Joaquin Valley. The company has provided traditional telephone solutions in the Fresno area for decades. In 1994, through a merger with McCaw Cellular Communications, Inc. (doing business as Cellular One), AT&T established a significant presence locally as the leading provider of cellular service and wireless business solutions. Committed to the community's business needs, AT&T employees also support many regional organizations and government entities, making important contributions to several area schools and educational programs.

The AT&T Cares program encourages employees to volunteer for community service by providing each employee with eight hours annually of paid time to volunteer at any charity or nonprofit organization. Since public and school safety are among the top issues facing the community, AT&T offers its services to help make the streets and neighborhoods safer places. Through the Safe School and Safe Streets programs, AT&T provides

cellular phones free of charge to schools and neighborhood watch groups. In addition, on-line resources provide connectivity and educational support to schools and communities, including free cable services in the classroom and information technology guides to help schools and communities use the Internet.

AT&T supports community events with an emphasis on diversity, youth, education, innovation and technology, and economic development. Some of the many events include the Hmong International New Year, the Hispanic Chamber's Women's and Business Conferences, the Fresno Metropolitan and the Fresno Art museums, the Fresno Philharmonic, the Boys and Girls Club, and the Fresno County Office of Education (FCOE) Academic Decathlon. The Fresno Chamber of Commerce, the Fresno Economic Development Corporation, and the Fresno Business Council also benefit from AT&T's community spirit.

State-of-the-art communications technology has revolutionized the way people conduct their daily business, and AT&T stands at the forefront of this industry. The company has the experience to incorporate the rapidly advancing multitude of technologies into a successful business strategy, connecting people throughout the world.

KJWL 99.3

THE ENTREPRENEURIAL SPIRIT IS ALIVE AND WELL IN FRESNO. IT's embodied in enterprises such as KJWL 99.3, the city's only locally owned radio station. ■ "Building KJWL has been a lifelong dream come true," says John Ostlund, who, along with his wife, Katie, owns the six-year-old station. "The buzz in the radio business nationwide is consolidation, but we plan to remain independent. By so doing, we can effectively focus our resources on our listeners, advertisers, and community organizations."

Despite stiff competition from network-owned properties in the Fresno market, KJWL has consistently remained among the city's top three stations. According to Ostlund, that's due in part to the station's unique format and audience demographics. "We average more than 60,000 listeners and we're the only local station playing music spanning six decades," he explains. "Our audience members can enjoy the vintage tunes of Nat King Cole and Frank Sinatra one minute, then hear contemporary artists like Barbra Streisand and Celine Dion the next. To accommodate our listeners' eclectic tastes, our music library has more than 5,000 titles."

MODEST BEGINNINGS

Ostlund's radio roots run deep. The 46-year-old Turlock native spent his high school days hanging out at KCEY radio as a weekend disc jockey before moving into sales. He later graduated to Fresno radio as a salesperson for Y94, but decided that a career in the advertising agency business would be more lucrative. In 1976, Ostlund founded Fresno Advertising Associates, which would become Jeffrey-Scott Advertising, Inc.(JSA)—named for his two nephews. Successful in its own right, JSA has grown into one of the valley's most prominent advertising, marketing, and public relations firms with annual capitalized billings of $9 million.

In the late 1980s, Ostlund decided to pursue his radio dream. After years of planning and preparation, KJWL officially went on the air on March 30, 1994, Ostlund's 41st birthday, with the classic tune "Unforgettable" by Nat King Cole.

Although Ostlund splits his time between the agency, the radio station, and his other passion, race car driving, KJWL General Manager Jeff Negrete oversees station operations on a full-time basis. Negrete is excited about KJWL's growth. Located in a renovated, 100-year-old warehouse in downtown Fresno, the station's floor space recently

expanded from 1,000 to 5,000 square feet.

"Building expansion is practically unheard of among stand-alone radio stations," notes Negrete, who came on board in October 1997. "We have recruited top-notch talent who put forth a great team effort, and we are all proud of the fact that we can compete effectively with the bigger stations in town." The facilities also offer enhanced production capabilities with two state-of-the-art digital studios and enough future space to "super-serve our audience and advertisers," adds Ostlund.

GIVING SOMETHING BACK

The station's commercial success is just one source of management pride. Ostlund and Negrete are truly at their best when they talk about nurturing local not-for-profit organizations. "Our mission is to embrace this city, because we feel an obligation to serve the community's best interests," says Ostlund, a past board member of the Fresno Revitalization Corporation.

"KJWL is a remarkable organization and a huge resource for us," says Susan Stiltz, executive director of Tree Fresno, a volunteer-based urban forestry program that has benefited from the station's promotional efforts, as well as from the staff's hands-on tree planting activities. "KJWL is associated with so many positive events in our community, and Fresno's citizens truly appreciate its involvement."

Tambra Bane, special events director for the Community Medical Foundation, was surprised when KJWL approached her organization about sponsoring an upcoming Sinatra tribute concert and donating the proceeds to the foundation. Organizers of the December 12 performance featuring

Las Vegas-based Sinatra "voice-alike" crooner Bobby Barrett hope to raise $30,000 for Community Medical Center's Regional Burn Center and Trauma Services.

"Jeff Negrete and the entire KJWL staff have taken the lead in this event and we are assisting them," Bane explains. "KJWL is known throughout Fresno for its integrity, and we are deeply touched by how they stepped up to the plate to organize this event for our patients' benefit."

Other local organizations have profited from KJWL's community commitment as well. A recent

station-sponsored golf tournament for St. Anthony's School netted more than $20,000 for the Catholic elementary school. Also, some 5,000 individuals attended a station-organized community job fair in spring 2000. And thanks to hourly public service announcements, dozens of not-for-profit agencies have a chance to convey their messages and needs to the listening audience.

KJWL is so involved for one simple reason: "We're just doing our share to help the community flourish," Ostlund says. "Fresno is a terrific city with a lot of promise. We're thrilled to be a part of its success."

KJWL's NEWLY DESIGNED OFFICE SPACE IN A DOWNTOWN FRESNO WAREHOUSE REPRESENTS A COMMITMENT TO THE CITY'S REDEVELOPMENT.

KJWL, FRESNO'S ONLY LOCALLY OWNED RADIO STATION, HAS CONSISTENTLY RANKED AMONG THE CITY'S TOP THREE STATIONS.

The Radisson Hotel & Conference Center

VISITORS ENTERING THE RADISSON HOTEL & CONFERENCE Center in downtown Fresno are instantly swept away by the world-class luxury, the impeccable service, and an eight-story atrium with a three-story waterfall. The atmosphere of elegance and convenience has been carefully cultivated to provide clients all the comforts of home, combined with all the amenities necessary for a memorable stay.

The Hotel Group of Scottsdale, Arizona, which took over the management of the hotel in 1999, is known for quality and high levels of service—the perfect candidate for the job of running the establishment. The staff of the Radisson Hotel embraces the high ideal of the building's owner, and has raised hotel standards in Fresno to a new level. A multiyear renovation is currently taking place, with features such as direct-dial phones and the most advanced voice mail system installed in every room.

SATISFYING EVERY NEED

One of our biggest selling points is our location. Not only is Fresno close to everything, it also has a lot to offer on its own," says General Manager Steven Klein. "People love the fact that in an hour, they can be skiing, or in just a couple of hours, they can be at the beach. We're located between two large metropolitan cities, and we have our own international airport to make for easy commuting."

Guests can enjoy the majestic scenery of the Sierra Nevada at two national forests and three national parks: Kings Canyon, Sequoia, and Yosemite. Fresno's location in the heart of California makes travel to and from many exciting destinations an easy day trip by automobile. Whether it is golf, water sports, skiing, hiking, antiquing, visiting world-class museums, or browsing around the nearby, unique shopping centers, the Radisson Hotel & Conference Center is the perfect facility for all occasions.

Making sure every convenience is available to its guests is the Radisson Hotel & Conference Center's main goal. Standards such as 27-inch televisions, cherrywood and mahogany hardwood furniture, hair dryers, coffeemakers, and irons and ironing boards, along with upgraded amenities such as armoires and desks with swivel chairs, are the little touches that make the Radisson Hotel & Conference Center complete.

Other special guest conveniences include complimentary shuttle service to Fresno Yosemite International Airport, free parking, exercise room, video game arcade, heated indoor/outdoor pool, Jacuzzi and sauna, newsstand and gift shop, complimentary safe-deposit boxes, valet dry cleaning, and full-service beauty salon. The Radisson's International Café is open from 6 a.m. to 10 p.m. daily, and features gourmet cuisine from around the world. Guests can also enjoy the spacious atrium and waterfall while relaxing with a beverage at the Atrium Lounge, open every day from noon to midnight.

AN IDEAL CONVENTION LOCATION

A first-class facility containing 321 rooms—including deluxe and presidential suites—the Radisson Hotel & Conference Center addresses the needs of the prime convention area for Central

VISITORS ENTERING THE RADISSON HOTEL & CONFERENCE CENTER IN DOWNTOWN FRESNO WILL BE INSTANTLY SWEPT AWAY BY THE WORLD-CLASS LUXURY, THE IMPECCABLE SERVICE, AND AN EIGHT-STORY ATRIUM WITH A THREE-STORY WATERFALL.

California. The growing number of conventions targeting Fresno has been a boon to the city's economy, and the Radisson has led the way in satisfying these clients' needs. As a result, nearly 60 percent of the hotel's business is derived from conventions.

The reason for the hotel's success in this arena is simple: As the largest full-service hotel and convention center in Central California, it has more than 24,000 square feet of meeting space available in its conference center, with adjustable configurations to include up to 18 separate rooms. Additional flexible meeting space is within walking distance of the hotel at the Fresno Convention Center.

Banquet facilities can accommodate up to 1,200 guests, and the on-site staff of event professionals helps clients with every aspect of a project. The new Sequoia Ballroom (formerly John Q's restaurant) has recently undergone a complete face-lift. The ballroom is now one of the most

▶ CARL F. LARSEN

elegant in the area, with seating space for up to 280 people for dining events or up to 400 for theater-style meetings. Whatever the event, and whatever the need, the hotel's convention staff can handle every detail.

"The Radisson is truly one of the premier convention facilities in the state of California," says Cheryl Capling, director of sales.

"We have conventions already booked for the next few years. People are excited about Fresno, and about bringing their businesses and their conventions here. We'll continue to work closely with the community to enhance Fresno and the Radisson."

Fresno has embraced the Radisson Hotel & Conference Center, and knows the owners and staff are serious about their investment in the city. This recognition has only strengthened the hotel's resolve to continue to strive for perfection. "With our renovations, aggressive marketing, and quality service, we are bringing great business to this town," says Klein. "The hotel stands proud with its reputation for quality and service, and is looking forward to a long and healthy partnership with Fresno."

THE RADISSON HOTEL & CONFERENCE CENTER'S BALLROOM IS THE LARGEST IN THE AREA.

THE INTERNATIONAL CAFÉ OFFERS ELEGANT DINING IN A CASUAL, FAMILY-ORIENTED SETTING (LEFT).

THE ATRIUM LOUNGE IS PERFECT FOR RELAXING (RIGHT).

Gap Inc.

IN 1999, CALIFORNIA-BASED GAP INC. OPENED A STATE-OF-THE-art regional distribution center in Fresno, greatly expanding the company's presence in the area well beyond its retail operations. This cutting-edge facility is a critical part of the company's international distribution network. Gap Inc. is a global specialty retailer with more than 111,000 employees worldwide, revenues exceeding $11.6 billion annually, and more than 2,900 stores in six countries.

Gap Inc. surveyed more than 100 locations west of the Rocky Mountains as potential sites for its Pacific Distribution Center. The company ultimately chose Fresno for the city's midstate location, ease of access to road and air transportation, and skilled labor pool. The partnership between state, city, and Gap Inc. officials made the Fresno distribution center a reality.

CLOCKWISE FROM TOP:
GAP INC. OPENED ITS PACIFIC DISTRIBUTION CENTER IN FRESNO IN MAY 1999.

GAP INC. IS INVESTING IN FRESNO IN MANY WAYS. OLD NAVY SPONSORS THE FRESNO GRIZZLIES AAA BASEBALL TEAM.

THE COMPANY'S STATE-OF-THE-ART FRESNO FACILITY HELPS GAP INC. GET ITEMS TO STORES AND RAPIDLY RESPOND TO MARKET DEMANDS.

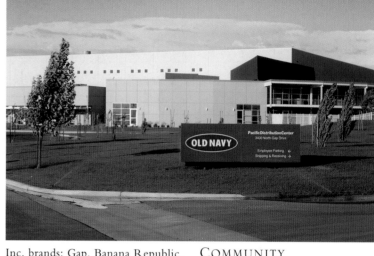

SUPPORTING FUTURE GROWTH

The opening of this facility comes at an important time, given the growth of all three Gap Inc. brands: Gap, Banana Republic, and Old Navy. In fact, the company has already announced plans to double the size of the center to roughly 1 million square feet in the fall of 2000—far ahead of initial company projections.

"Fresno worked hard to make sure it could compete with communities from across the western United States for distribution industry business," notes Don Fisher, Gap Inc. founder and chairman of the board. "We're looking forward to a long and mutually beneficial relationship with the city, its leaders, and its residents."

COMMUNITY INVOLVEMENT

Gap Inc. is dedicated to investing in the Fresno community, from hiring local construction contractors and employees to funding education programs and a local Boys and Girls Club project. Old Navy is also a proud sponsor of the hometown AAA baseball team, the Fresno Grizzlies.

Gap Inc. believes that being a good neighbor is part of doing good business, and Fresno offers ample opportunities for both the company and its employees to get involved. For Gap Inc., Fresno feels like home.

ARBUTUS
UNEEDO
(STRAWBERRY)

BEGINNING AS A SMALL PUBLISHER OF LOCAL NEWSPAPERS IN the 1930s, Towery Publishing, Inc. today produces a wide range of community-oriented materials, including books (Urban Tapestry Series), business directories, magazines, and Internet publications. Building on its long heritage of excellence, the company has become global in scope, with cities from San Diego to Sydney represented by Towery products. In all its endeavors, this Memphis-based company strives to be synonymous with service, utility, and quality.

A DIVERSITY OF COMMUNITY-BASED PRODUCTS

Over the years, Towery has become the largest producer of published materials for North American chambers of commerce. From membership directories that enhance business-to-business communication to visitor and relocation guides tailored to reflect the unique qualities of the communities they cover, the company's chamber-oriented materials offer comprehensive information on dozens of topics, including housing, education, leisure activities, health care, and local government.

In 1998, the company acquired Cincinnati-based Target Marketing, an established provider of detailed city street maps to more than 200 chambers of commerce throughout the United States and Canada. Now a division of Towery, Target offers full-color maps that include local landmarks and points of interest, such as parks, shopping centers, golf courses, schools, industrial parks, city and county limits, subdivision names, public buildings, and even block numbers on most streets.

In 1990, Towery launched the Urban Tapestry Series, an award-winning collection of oversized, hardbound photojournals detailing the people, history, culture, environment, and commerce of various metropolitan areas. These coffee-table books highlight a community through three basic elements: an introductory essay by a noted local individual; an exquisite collection of four-color photographs; and profiles of the companies and organizations that animate the area's business life.

To date, more than 80 Urban Tapestry Series editions have been published in cities around the world, from New York to Vancouver to Sydney. Authors of the books' introductory essays include former U.S. President Gerald Ford (Grand Rapids), former Alberta Premier Peter Lougheed (Calgary), CBS anchor Dan Rather (Austin), ABC anchor Hugh Downs (Phoenix), best-selling mystery author Robert B. Parker (Boston), American Movie Classics host Nick Clooney (Cincinnati), Senator Richard Lugar (Indianapolis), and Challenger Center founder June Scobee Rodgers (Chattanooga).

To maintain hands-on quality in all of its periodicals and books, Towery has long used the latest production methods available. The company was the first production environment in the United States to combine desktop publishing with color separations and image scanning to produce finished film suitable for burning plates for four-color printing. Today, Towery relies on state-of-the-art digital prepress services to produce more than 8,000 pages each year, containing well over 30,000 high-quality color images.

AN INTERNET PIONEER

By combining its long-standing expertise in community-oriented published materials with advanced production capabilities, a global sales force, and extensive data management expertise, Towery has emerged as a significant provider

TOWERY PUBLISHING PRESIDENT AND CEO J. ROBERT TOWERY HAS EXPANDED THE BUSINESS HIS PARENTS STARTED IN THE 1930S TO INCLUDE A GROWING ARRAY OF TRADITIONAL AND ELECTRONIC PUBLISHED MATERIALS, AS WELL AS INTERNET AND MULTIMEDIA SERVICES, THAT ARE MARKETED LOCALLY, NATIONALLY, AND INTERNATIONALLY.

STEVE DAVIS

of Internet-based city information. In keeping with its overall focus on community resources, the company's Internet efforts represent a natural step in the evolution of the business.

The primary product lines within the Internet division are the introCity™ sites. Towery's introCity sites introduce newcomers, visitors, and longtime residents to every facet of a particular community, while simultaneously placing the local chamber of commerce at the forefront of the city's Internet activity. The sites include newcomer information, calendars, photos, citywide business listings with everything from nightlife to shopping to family fun, and online maps pinpointing the exact location of businesses, schools, attractions, and much more.

DECADES OF PUBLISHING EXPERTISE

In 1972, current President and CEO J. Robert Towery succeeded his parents in managing the printing and publishing business they had founded nearly four decades earlier. Soon thereafter, he expanded the scope of the company's published materials to include *Memphis* magazine and other successful regional and national

publications. In 1985, after selling its locally focused assets, Towery began the trajectory on which it continues today, creating community-oriented materials that are often produced in conjunction with chambers of commerce and other business organizations.

Despite the decades of change, Towery himself follows a long-standing family philosophy of unmatched service and unflinching quality. That approach extends throughout the entire organization to include more than 120 employees at the Memphis headquarters, another 80 located in Northern Kentucky outside Cincinnati, and more than 40 sales, marketing, and editorial staff traveling to and working in a growing list of client cities. All of its products, and more information about the company, are featured on the Internet at www.towery.com.

In summing up his company's steady growth, Towery restates the essential formula that has driven the business since its first pages were published: "The creative energies of our staff drive us toward innovation and invention. Our people make the highest possible demands on themselves, so I know that our future is secure if the ingredients for success remain a focus on service and quality."

TOWERY PUBLISHING WAS THE FIRST PRODUCTION ENVIRONMENT IN THE UNITED STATES TO COMBINE DESKTOP PUBLISHING WITH COLOR SEPARATIONS AND IMAGE SCANNING TO PRODUCE FINISHED FILM SUITABLE FOR BURNING PLATES FOR FOUR-COLOR PRINTING. TODAY, THE COMPANY'S STATE-OF-THE-ART NETWORK OF MACINTOSH AND WINDOWS WORKSTATIONS ALLOWS IT TO PRODUCE MORE THAN 8,000 PAGES EACH YEAR, CONTAINING WELL OVER 30,000 HIGH-QUALITY COLOR IMAGES (TOP).

THE TOWERY FAMILY'S PUBLISHING ROOTS CAN BE TRACED TO 1935, WHEN R.W. TOWERY (FAR LEFT) BEGAN PRODUCING A SERIES OF COMMUNITY HISTORIES IN TENNESSEE, MISSISSIPPI, AND TEXAS. THROUGHOUT THE COMPANY'S HISTORY, THE FOUNDING FAMILY HAS CONSISTENTLY EXHIBITED A COMMITMENT TO CLARITY, PRECISION, INNOVATION, AND VISION (BOTTOM).

Photographers

Allsport was founded the moment freelance photographer Tony Duffy captured the now-famous picture of Bob Beamon breaking the world long-jump record at the Mexico City Olympics in 1968. Originally headquartered in London, Allsport has expanded to include offices in New York and Los Angeles. Its pictures have appeared in every major publication in the world, and the best of its portfolio has been displayed at elite photographic exhibitions at the Royal Photographic Society and the Olympic Museum in Lausanne.

Point Anderson lives in Squaw Valley in the foothills of the Sierra Nevadas. He has traveled and photographed extensively all over the American West and Alaska, taking an especially close look at the Anasazi dwellings of the Southwest. He operates Points Photography, a library of medium- and large-format images of scenic landscapes of the western United States.

Chris Auger, a Schenevus, New York, native, graduated from Texas A&M University with a degree in geography and environmental studies. He now lives in Ft. Worth, where he is the owner and operator of Auger Photography. Auger specializes in outdoor and travel photography and has a client list that includes *Rolling Stone* and Scope Enterprises.

© JONATHAN POSTAL / TOWERY PUBLISHING, INC.

Pete Cervantes is a Fresno native and graduate of Fresno City College. He picked up photography as a hobby two years ago and has since produced work for Fresno Christmas benefits and area jazz festivals.

George Flint Jr. is a former schoolteacher in the Fresno Unified School District. Since his retirement in 1991, he has traveled extensively, photographing landscapes, still lifes, and close-ups of flowers. Flint's work has been exhibited in one-person and group shows in Fresno at Spectrum Gallery, several savings and loans, the Saroyan Theater, and the President's Gallery at California State University, Fresno.

Carol Hunt, a Santa Fe resident, is employed by St. Francis Hospital. She concentrates her photography on the people and culture of northern New Mexico, sports, high-rise buildings, and churches.

Michael Karibian is a self-employed photographer specializing in commercial photography and graphic design. He has a bachelor's degree in art from California State University, Fresno, and a master's degree in art from California State University, San Francisco. Karibian has 25 years of photography experience and has produced editorial, advertising, corporate, and public relations work.

Marilynn "Mimi" Mann is a former real estate broker and residential appraiser who now focuses her time on photography. She has a bachelor of arts degree in social science from California State University, and is taking photography classes to perfect her skill.

Lupe Mora immigrated to Fresno from Michoacán, Mexico, in 1972. She attended California State University, Fresno, receiving degrees in photojournalism, French, and art. She is now the owner and operator of Lupe Mora Photography and specializes in commercial, editorial, and human interest photography. Mora has photographed for The Guinness Book of World Records, *Farandula International*, Mervyns, and Mars Records.

Tom and Sally Myers have been full-time freelance photographers for 30 years, and have been published in many magazines, including *National Geographic, National Wildlife, Newsweek*, and *Animals* (London), as well as in Towery Publishing's *New York: A State of Mind* and *Sacramento Tapestry*. Their photos appear in books and educational CD-ROM materials throughout the world, in addition to advertisements, album covers, and Hallmark cards and calendars. With their son, **Jeff Myers**, the family has more than 400,000 color images in its files, covering a variety of geographic areas, including Europe, the Pacific Coast from Mexico to Alaska, and inland to Colorado.

Judi Parks is an award-winning photojournalist living and working in the San Francisco Bay Area. Her educational background spans anthropology, photography, international conflict resolution, and clinical psychology. Parks' work has been collected by numerous museums and public collections in the United States and Europe. Her documentary series *Home Sweet Home: Caring for America's Elderly* was recently honored with the *Communication Arts-Design Annual* 1999 Award of Excellence for an unpublished series. Parks is also a professional writer, with articles appearing in more than 40 newspapers and magazines.

Kelly Petersen is a commercial photographer with specializations in advertising and marketing. Originally from Salt Lake City, she moved to Fresno in 1979 after completing her education at the University of Utah and Brigham Young University.

Photophile, established in San Diego in 1967, is owned and operated by Nancy Likins-Masten. An internationally known stock photography agency, Photophile houses more than a million color images and represents more than 90 contributing local and international photographers. Subjects include extensive coverage of the West Coast, business/industry, people/lifestyles, health/medicine, travel, scenics, wildlife, and adventure sports, plus 200 additional categories.

Corey Rich is an adventure sports photographer with clients ranging from Patagonia and Oakley to Quokka Sports and *Outside Magazine*. With a bachelor of arts degree from Fresno State University, Rich is the owner and operator of Coreyography.

Marc Strickland, a Fresno native, is a self-taught photographer who specializes in nature and photojournalism. He is currently traveling the world to build his photography portfolio in hopes of working for *National Geographic*.

Index of Profiles

◆ © TIM FLEMING

Library of Congress Cataloging-in-Publication Data

Fresno : heartbeat of the valley / introduction by Cruz M. Bustamante ; art direction by
Enrique Espinosa ; sponsored by the Fresno Chamber of Commerce.

    p. cm. — (Urban tapestry series)

   Includes index.

    ISBN 1-881096-80-7 (alk. paper)

     1. Fresno (Calif.)—Civilization. 2. Fresno (Calif.)—Pictorial works. 3. Fresno
(Calif.)—Economic conditions. 4. Business enterprises—California—Fresno. I
Bustamante, Cruz M., 1953- II. Fresno Chamber of Commerce. III. Series.

F869.F8 F74 2000

979.4'83—dc21

00-036449

Towery Publishing, Inc., The Towery Building, 1835 Union Avenue, Memphis, TN 38104

Publisher: J. Robert Towery ❖ Executive Publisher: Jenny McDowell ❖ National Sales Manager: Stephen Hung
Marketing Director: Carol Culpepper ❖ Project Directors: Ron Calabrese, Andrea Glazier, Mel Merck, and Mike
Muesser ❖ Executive Editor: David B. Dawson ❖ Managing Editor: Lynn Conlee ❖ Senior Editor: Carlisle Hacker
Editor/Profile Manager: Brian Johnston ❖ Editors: Jay Adkins, Stephen M. Deusner, Ginny Reeves ❖ Editor/Caption
Writer: Sunni Thompson ❖ Copy Editors: Rebecca Green, Danna Greenfield ❖ Editorial Assistant: Andrew Harlow
❖ Profile Writer: Kerry Aller ❖ Creative Director: Brian Groppe ❖ Photography Editor: Jonathan
Postal ❖ Photographic Consultant: Rodney Gavroian ❖ Profile Designers: Laurie Beck, Melissa Ellis, Laura Higley
❖ Production Manager: Brenda Pattat ❖ Photography Coordinator: Robin Lankford ❖ Production Assistants:
Robert Barnett, Loretta Lane ❖ Digital Color Supervisor: Darin Ipema ❖ Digital Color Technicians: Eric Friedl,
Deidre Kesler, Brent Salazar, Mark Svetz ❖ Production Resources Manager: Dave Dunlap Jr. ❖ Print Coordinator:
Beverly Timmons ❖

Printed in China